Author's Note

Welcome, and thank you for choosing the **Lead Guitar Book Bundle**.

Want to kick-start your lead guitar playing? You've just made the first important step! This value pack is an all-in-one compilation of three individual guitar books. While these books can be read as stand-alone guides, they were written to complement one another. Together they provide a comprehensive blueprint for developing your understanding of lead guitar and enhancing your playing skills.

Here's an overview of each book included in this bundle:

1. **Lead Guitar Breakthrough** offers a collection of essential lessons that guide you step-by-step through key concepts for overcoming obstacles in your lead playing. This book provides a fundamental system for fretboard navigation as well as the tools needed to cultivate your own style and musicality.

2. **Learn Your Guitar Scales** provides an in-depth introduction to the fundamental patterns that underpin everything we do on guitar. This handbook includes specific tips and exercises for applying this information practically. Beyond simply demonstrating what these shapes look like, this book explores the sound, structure, and common uses for each pattern in context.

3. **5-Minute Guitar Jams** features a collection of high-quality jam tracks for practicing improvisation, scales, and other technical exercises. This guide takes a detailed look at multiple chord progressions, outlines numerous scale options for improvising, and discusses various concepts for getting the most out of practicing with jam tracks.

Although it isn't necessary to read these books in sequence, you'll find that they're placed in a logical order. First, **Lead Guitar Breakthrough** guides you through the fundamentals of mastering fretboard navigation, understanding theory, and developing your playing technique. Then, **Learn Your Guitar Scales** provides a detailed reference guide for consolidating and moving beyond the key concepts presented in the first book. Finally, **5-Minute Guitar Jams** offers a handy practice companion for the material covered in the previous two books, helping you to apply these insights creatively and gain more from your practice time.

You can choose to work through this bundle methodically from start to finish, or use it more casually as a reference guide. A recommended starting point is to spend a small amount of time browsing through each book. Once you're familiar with the scope of the material, simply progress through it at your own pace. Focus on the sections that seem most relevant to you, and take note of those you'd like to explore at a later time. Ultimately, how you use this resource is up to you. Don't be afraid to mix things up, moving between different books and chapters. You're in control of your own learning, so be sure to do it in a way that makes sense to you!

I sincerely hope the insights within these pages can play a meaningful part in your becoming the guitar player you've always wanted to be.

—Luke Zecchin

Getting lost on the guitar neck?
Finally, fretboard memorization made easy!

If you like this bundle, you'll love our *Fretboard Memorization Workshop*! This online master class is your shortcut to demystifying the fretboard puzzle. Here you'll be guided step-by-step through the key concepts, techniques, and exercises needed to master your entire fretboard—quickly and easily. These insights have helped thousands of students worldwide, and we're certain they'll help you too!

For more information, head to **LearnYourFretboard.com**.

Quick Navigation Menu

Get Your Free Online Bonus Now!

This bundle comes complete with free online bonus material. We've compiled companion websites to enhance your reading experience. Extras include audio examples, backing tracks, bonus downloads, and more!

Get your free bonus content at: **www.guitariq.com/lgbb-bonus**

LEAD GUITAR BREAKTHROUGH

Essential Lessons

FRETBOARD NAVIGATION, THEORY & TECHNIQUE

LUKE ZECCHIN

This book is dedicated to my beautiful wife Jasmin. Through the seasons you are evergreen.

Published by **GuitarIQ.com**

Copyedited by Allister Thompson

Proofread by Dan Foster

Illustrated by Jasmin Zecchin

Contents

Preface

Welcome, and thank you for choosing **Lead Guitar Breakthrough**.

Although we often teach music in a linear and methodical way, in reality, for many guitar players this doesn't necessarily reflect the way we learn. Our approach is usually far more *circular*. We piece bits of information together as we go, learning different songs, riffs, shapes, and techniques, constantly revisiting things as our skills improve. While there's nothing wrong with this approach, it has the tendency to leave us with isolated bits of seemingly unrelated information. We may know how to play certain things on the guitar but find it hard to understand how all the pieces fit together.

This book is a resource for those eager to improve their lead guitar skills. However, it wasn't written merely to demonstrate popular guitar licks, show you how to play in one particular style, or break down the solos of your favorite players (although it may inadvertently assist in those pursuits). Here we're concerned with the bigger picture. The essential function of this book is to provide a road map for understanding how things are connected on the fretboard. As such, we'll establish a fundamental framework for navigating the entire guitar neck. This will in turn assist you in developing speed and fluidity in your playing, understanding key centers, using chord progressions, building melodic ideas, and more.

Put simply, this is the book I wish I'd read much earlier in my guitar playing journey. While there are no overnight shortcuts to becoming an accomplished musician, working from a solid foundation will significantly help streamline this process. May this information prove as valuable to you as it has been to me.

I sincerely hope this book sparks a breakthrough in your own playing and becomes a catalyst for continued discovery and inspiration.

—Luke Zecchin

Introduction

Developing a solid understanding of the fundamentals is invaluable for musicians of any skill level. While this book is a resource for guitar players at various stages in their ability, it was primarily written for those wanting more from their lead playing. As I already alluded to, the focus here isn't solely on how to *do* specific things technically. The primary interest is how to *think* about the things we do creatively.

As stated, this book aims to provide a road map for navigating the fretboard. Drawing on this analogy, a map exists to give us context. It shows us where to go and how best to get there. However, it also assists in two other equally important pursuits: *exploration* and *discovery*. This resource presents a concise and easy-to-follow approach to becoming a more complete guitar player. Above all, though, its most valuable contribution will hopefully be to encourage you to think creatively for yourself.

It's always important to remember that while others may be responsible for the teaching, you're ultimately responsible for the learning. Here we're concerned with the essential concepts for a well-rounded approach to lead guitar playing. The way you experiment with and apply that information is up to you. A book of this nature will necessarily include numerous exercises and practical tips. However, you should always place more value on the concepts (and how they can be applied or adapted elsewhere) rather than the specific exercises or techniques themselves.

Additionally, this content may introduce you to techniques that could feel foreign at first. Remember to take regular playing breaks and be conscious of fatigue or excessive tension in the hands, arms, shoulders, and neck. In keeping with this, the set tempos of each exercise in this book serve only as general suggestions. All exercises should be played at a comfortable tempo that facilitates accuracy. Lastly, it's extremely important to work through the information presented here at your own pace. The measure of a lesson's value is never how quickly you learn something but how well you learn it.

Tips on Technique

Before we begin, it seems appropriate to briefly cover some basics concerning guitar technique. Admittedly, differences in body type, playing style, and personal preference (among other variables) make it difficult to define a one-size-fits-all approach to playing technique. An overly simple yet still fitting definition of good technique is our ability to maximize *tone* while minimizing *tension*. That is, we're endeavoring to play with fluency, clarity, and accuracy in a way that feels comfortable and natural.

Ideally, playing guitar should feel as effortless as possible. Effortlessness, however, requires practice. It's a byproduct of reliable and efficient technique. With this in mind, here are some key things to consider as you work through this book:

- **Choose a Comfortable Playing Position:** The height and angle of your guitar directly impact the effectiveness of your playing technique. Ideally, your guitar neck should be elevated at a comfortable angle and stay at approximately the same height whether you're sitting or standing.

- **Be Mindful of Your Posture:** Slouching and staying relaxed aren't the same thing. It's very difficult to keep the tension out of your neck, shoulders, and back if you have a tendency to sit awkwardly or hunch over while playing.

- **Relax and Remember to Breathe:** Many guitar players find concentration comes at the expense of forgetting to breathe naturally. This leads to unnecessary tightness and isn't conducive to good technique. Seek to maintain relaxed hands, wrists, and forearms at all times.

- **Avoid Unnecessary Wrist Tension:** Your wrists should stay relatively straight in line with your forearms; this is the position in which they're most comfortable. It's increasingly difficult to move your hands and fingers freely if your wrists are bent at unnatural angles.

- **Monitor Your Thumb Position:** Ideally, for general playing your thumb should sit upright, comfortably across from your 1st finger behind the guitar neck. Raising it too high over the top of the guitar neck will affect the mobility and natural curve of your fingers.

- **Use Your Fingertips:** Unless you're holding down multiple strings, avoid using the pads of your fingers on the fretboard. Allow each finger to angle in comfortably (keeping with their natural curve) and target the area around your fingertips for improved accuracy and control.

- **Gauge Your Pressure:** It's often surprising how little pressure is needed to sound a note cleanly. Remember, there's only a small distance between the bottom of a string and the top of a fret. Avoiding excess pressure will increase speed and agility.

- **Minimize Your Movements:** There's no benefit in unnecessary effort. Keeping fingers close to the fretboard and reducing picking action avoids exaggerating the movement required by either hand. Economizing your technique will help improve speed and consistency.

- **Focus on Efficient Picking:** There'll be less resistance in your picking technique if the guitar pick is positioned at a slight but consistent angle to the strings (not flat or parallel). Play using only the tip of the pick, holding it securely but not tightly for smooth and controlled picking strokes.

- **Listen to Your Body:** Your body will tell you if it's tense or uncomfortable. Listen to it. If playing guitar is painful, you're likely not doing it right. Use any warning signs as an opportunity to reassess the effectiveness of your playing technique. Obviously, seek professional medical advice if required.

1

Major Building Blocks

In this first chapter, we take an in-depth look at the major scale and its importance in lead guitar playing.

Introduction

In this first section, we'll start by getting our basic musical bearings. This information will be foundational not only to everything covered in this book but also to our general musical understanding. When endeavoring to understand the bigger picture, we must begin with a solid reference point on which to build our overarching framework. In light of this, it's difficult to think of a better starting point for guitar players than the major scale. Chords, pentatonic scales, modes, and arpeggios, for example, are all contained within the major scale. Even musical information that moves outside the major scale structure is still defined by the way it differs from this scale. Simply put, the major scale is a vital part of the fabric holding music together. As such, it should be our first stop when seeking to make sense of the guitar fretboard.

Our Reference Point

First, let's establish what a major scale looks and sounds like on guitar. Here we have a basic single-octave major scale in the key of G. This scale shape is likely already familiar to a lot of guitar players. Even those who don't know this shape should still find the sound easily recognizable:

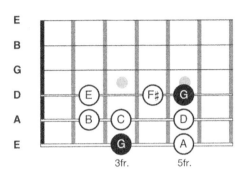

Exercise 1.1

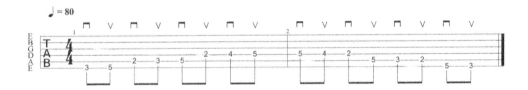

Note: We'll use G major for the purpose of illustration, but these same patterns and shapes can be shifted up or down to be played in any key.

In order for us to make practical use of this information, let's take a closer look at how a major scale is built. If, for example, we take this same G major scale and lay the notes out horizontally across the low E string, we discover two important things:

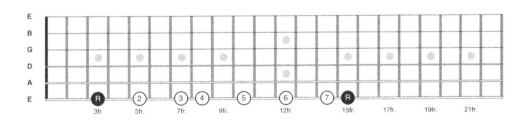

- First, the guitar is an instrument that allows us to play the same thing in multiple ways. This is certainly a recurring theme when learning guitar, and it hints at how we might begin to use the fretboard more comprehensively in our playing. Specific chords and scales aren't limited to one particular shape or position on the guitar neck; rather, they can be expressed in various forms across the fretboard.

- Second, if we attribute a number to each note of the scale, ascending from the root note as demonstrated, we see the essential structure common to all major scales. A major scale is basically a series of whole-step (two-fret) movements. The only exceptions to this are after the 3rd and 7th notes of the scale. These both ascend by a single half step (one fret). This is the foundational formula that's found in all major scales, regardless of their key or starting position. Just knowing this one simple principle immediately gives us the ability to build a major scale from any note, on any string, across the whole fretboard!

Tip: Picturing the major scale is like visualizing an eight-step ladder. The third and seventh steps are just half the distance closer than all the others.

Why is this important for improving our playing? As already highlighted, chords and scales can be played in many different ways across the guitar neck. What becomes essential is developing a system or structure that provides a foundation for visualizing, sorting through, and understanding all the musical information available to us. Since the major scale is central to everything in Western music, it makes sense that this would be the core framework we'd reference on the fretboard.

In other words, once we understand how the major scale is built, we can see that there's an inherent structure or pattern running across the entire fretboard. This is true in all keys, regardless of string or neck position. This structure provides the road map for navigating the fretboard, irrespective of what we're playing or the key we're playing in.

Tip: Even though looking at the fretboard can initially seem overwhelming, remember that we're only dealing with 12 notes. These notes repeat themselves in a consistent and predictable fashion across the guitar neck. Keeping this in mind will make the fretboard seem significantly more manageable.

Our Starting Point

Although it may not yet seem like much, the basic structure we've just looked at is foundational to all popular music. We've established that in any key there's a consistent pattern across all strings. The task now becomes finding the best way to organize this information into more easily understandable sections. This process will become clearer in the next chapter.

Before delving into how all the pieces fit together, let's begin by checking out the first scale pattern we'll use as our starting point:

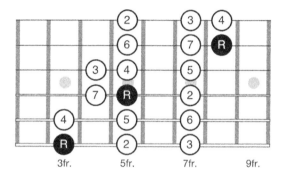

Exercise 1.2

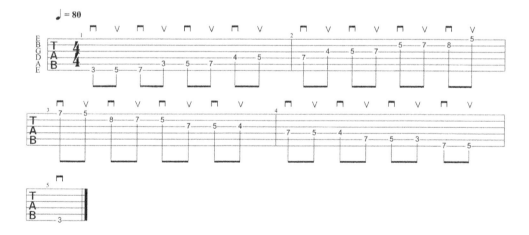

You can see that we're using the same major scale as before, but here it's being played in a different way. We're now spanning this scale across multiple octaves and are playing it in a way that places three notes on each string. This hints at the two real benefits to this approach:

- First, spanning a shape over multiple octaves maximizes the reach of that pattern within a single playing position. Put simply, we have more fretboard real estate available to us within a single area.

- Second, using three notes per string allows us to easily incorporate a wider range of techniques (such as economy picking or legato) into our playing. As we'll see in later chapters, this becomes an intuitive way of structuring melodic ideas for those who want to develop more speed and fluidity in their playing.

Note: Additionally, this scale shape highlights the three basic patterns our fingers will encounter when playing three notes per string in this way. They're as follows:

- Three notes separated by a whole step each (W/W).

- Three notes separated by a half step and then a whole step (H/W).

- Three notes separated by a whole step and then a half step (W/H).

For this scale and subsequent scales in this book, the suggested left-hand fingerings are:

- Using the 1st, 2nd, and 4th fingers for both W/W and H/W movements.

- Using the 1st, 3rd, and 4th fingers for W/H movements.

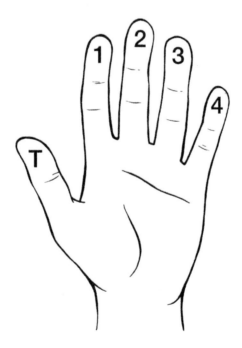

Tip: Built from the G note on the 3rd fret of the low E string, this scale pattern represents G major. If we built this shape from the F note on the 1st fret of the same string, our key center would logically change to F major. As such, learning to refer to notes by their respective numbers (often called degrees) will be of great benefit. Each number references a note's distance from the root note, or rather, its interval relationship to the root note. Although scale notes will change depending on the key we're playing in, the scale pattern will stay the same. In other words, in moving this shape around the guitar neck, the intervals stay the same regardless of the notes they represent.

Warming Up

For guitarists new to lead playing or who are mainly used to pentatonic scales, playing three notes per string can seem difficult at first. Below is a basic exercise to help familiarize our fingers with this new way of playing.

Note: It's important to use specific finger positions to maximize the effectiveness of this exercise. The initial line below should be played using the 1st and 2nd fingers. The middle line should be played using the 2nd and 4th fingers. And the last line should be played using the 1st and 4th fingers.

Exercise 1.3

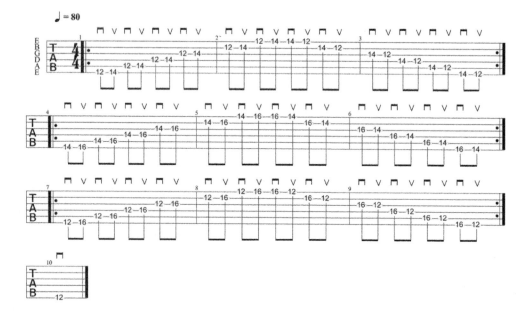

Tip: Once this feels comfortable and fluent, work on moving this exercise down toward the 1st fret. Focus on doing this one fret at a time to help your fingers adjust to the wider spacing at lower frets.

Focus Points

- Become familiar with the basic formula of how a major scale is built. Understand that in any given key this formula simply repeats across each string horizontally, just from different starting points in the scale.

- Focus on the outlined major scale shape (using three notes per string) until playing it feels controlled and natural. Experiment with shifting this scale shape around the guitar neck in different keys.

- Make use of the warm-up exercise provided as a way to build greater strength and dexterity in the left hand.

2

Seven Essential Shapes

Having centered our focus on the major scale, now we'll discuss its wider implications for fretboard navigation.

Introduction

In the previous chapter, we discussed how the major scale is central to almost everything else in music. We established that understanding the way this scale is built gives us a road map for navigating through any key across the entire fretboard. This provides a foundational reference point for understanding and communicating our musical ideas in any position on the guitar neck. In this chapter, we further unpack this concept, demonstrating how to view this information practically on the fretboard and providing the tools to begin piecing everything together.

Laying the Foundations

As previously stated, the major scale provides an inherent structure that runs across the entire guitar neck. Below are two diagrams demonstrating what the notes of a major scale look like when mapped across the complete fretboard. These examples again use the G major scale. As already established, this pattern is the same in any key, because the major scale structure doesn't change. For example, if we wanted to play in the key of A, this entire pattern would just shift up a whole step. The highlighted root notes would then align with A, not G:

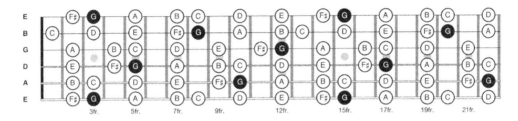

This second diagram mirrors the first but alternatively represents each note by its relative number. You can see that the ascending pattern is consistent on all strings. Each individual string just starts from a different point in the scale:

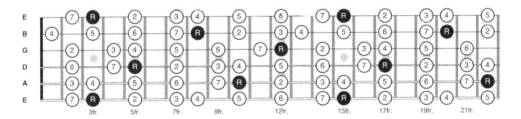

Admittedly, when we map out notes like this, it can look fairly complex at first. As we'll see, the real trick is to visualize the various parts that make up the whole. This involves isolating the smaller scale shapes found within this larger framework.

Tip: Remember, because the notes on a guitar repeat from the 12th fret, the bottom half of the guitar neck is the same as the top half. This means that any pattern across the fretboard is only half as complicated as it first appears.

The Modal Framework

It's helpful at this point to introduce a brief discussion on the *modes* of the major scale. You may have heard this term before. What exactly are the modes, and how are they relevant? Even though there seems to be a little confusion surrounding the topic of modes, the basic concept is relatively simple. Essentially, modes can be understood as inversions or alternate voicings of the major scale. In other words, modes use the same notes as the major scale they relate to, but they're built from different starting points within that scale. This will become clearer as we move through this chapter.

Understood fully, the modes of the major scale can function as unique scales within their own right. Each mode has its own unique flavor or tonal characteristic that sets it apart from the others. A more advanced application of the modes opens some interesting and creative possibilities for songwriting and improvisation. This is precisely why they're so popular among many guitar players.

Even without an in-depth understanding of modal theory, however, this concept is still very useful. This book is concerned with laying solid foundations on which to build our understanding. In the context of fretboard navigation, each mode can function as an alternate position of the major scale as we move around the guitar neck.

Thus far, we've seen how a major scale is built and what it looks like when mapped across the entire fretboard. If the task is to divide this information into smaller, more digestible sections, it's hard to think of a better system than the modal framework. To do this, visualize once again the notes of a major scale laid out horizontally across the low E string (demonstrated in **Chapter 1**). We'll now start building alternate positions of this scale, starting from each degree.

Note: For a more in-depth discussion on understanding and using modes, please refer to my book **Learn Your Guitar Scales**.

Shape 1

The good news is you already know the 1st position:

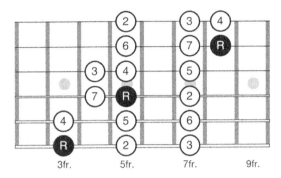

As we've seen, this is the 1st position of the major scale. Alternatively, you may have traditionally heard it referred to as the *Ionian* mode.

Exercise 2.1

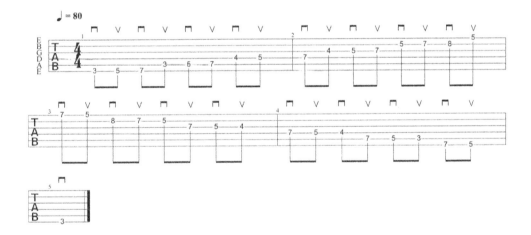

Note: When demonstrating a scale, it's common to extend it from one root note to another. Since the purpose here is to cover as much ground as possible, we're adding more notes from the scale on the high E string. While it's useful to visualize all three extra notes, only two of them will be used in these exercises.

Shape 2

Now let's take a look at the next scale position, starting from the 5th fret:

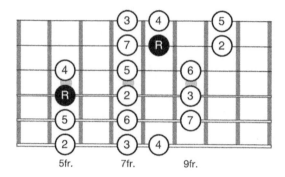

Here we have the 2nd position of the G major scale. Built from the 2nd degree, traditionally this scale could also be referred to as the *Dorian* mode.

Exercise 2.2

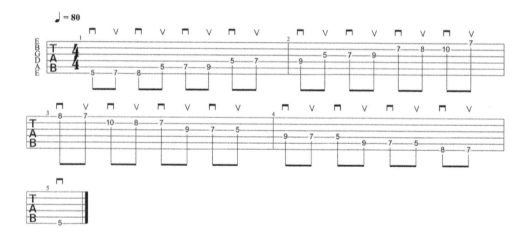

Note: Correctly represented in its modal context, this would be the A Dorian scale, meaning A would be represented as the root note or 1st degree. This would subsequently change the interval relationship (or numbers) for the rest of the notes, even though the pattern itself wouldn't change. However, because we're primarily treating these shapes as alternate positions of G major, we'll continue referencing G as our root note throughout these examples.

Shape 3

Here we have the next position, starting at the 7th fret:

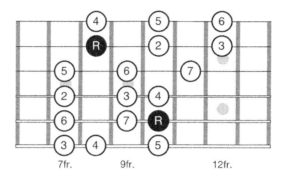

This is the 3rd position of the G major scale. Built from the 3rd degree, this scale could also be referred to as the *Phrygian* mode.

Exercise 2.3

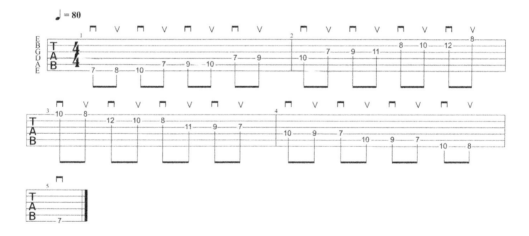

Shape 4

This is the next shape, starting at the 8th fret:

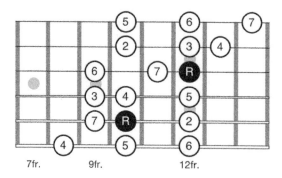

Here we have the 4th position of the G major scale. This scale is built from the 4th degree and is commonly referred to as the *Lydian* mode.

Exercise 2.4

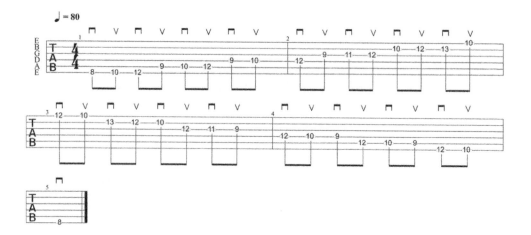

Shape 5

The next pattern starts from the 10th fret:

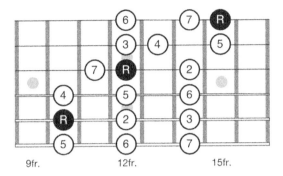

9fr.   12fr.   15fr.

This is the 5th position of G major. It's built from the 5th degree of the scale and is also referred to as the *Mixolydian* mode.

Exercise 2.5

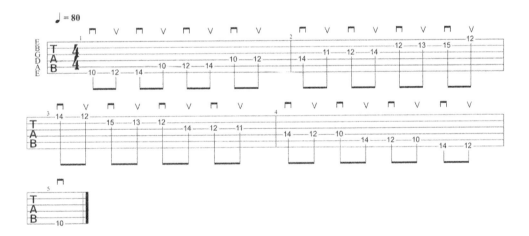

Shape 6

Here's the next position, starting at the 12th fret:

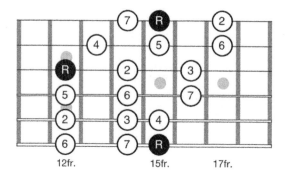

This is the 6th position of G major. We build this scale from the 6th degree, and it's also known as the *Aeolian* mode.

Exercise 2.6

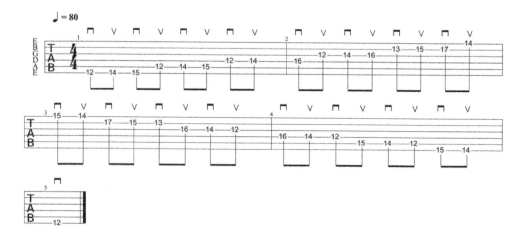

Note: This scale is also commonly referred to as the *natural minor* scale. Although we're using the notes of G major, when we start at the 6th degree we actually build an E minor scale. This hints at the way modes function. They shift the tonal center of one scale and in doing so create another scale.

> *Tip: As we'll see, each pattern functions in the context of both major and minor keys. This means these major scale patterns aren't limited to use over major progressions when we're songwriting or improvising.*

Shape 7

Lastly, we have the next position, starting from the 14th fret:

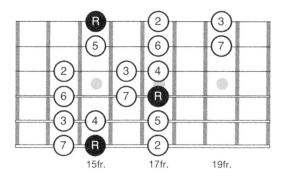

This is the 7th and final position of G major. We build this scale from the 7th degree, and it's alternatively known as the *Locrian* mode.

Exercise 2.7

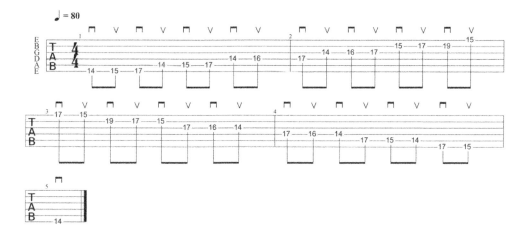

Putting It All Together

Compare each shape in the previous sections with the full-scale diagrams at the beginning of this chapter. What do you notice? The entire guitar neck has been covered by these seven shapes, repeating in sequence. Don't underestimate how valuable this information will become. We aren't learning scales for the purpose of just *learning scales*! We learn them because they provide an essential blueprint for playing over any key, in any position on the fretboard. Therefore, it's important to focus on memorizing each shape separately before moving on to the next position.

Once comfortable playing each position, it's helpful to practice moving through each pattern in sequence. You can do this simply by playing through one position several times before ascending to the next position and repeating the process.

Note: Remember to make use of the recommended fingerings in **Chapter 1** for each scale shape. Basic alternate down/up picking strokes have been suggested for these exercises. However, as we'll see, once you become more comfortable with these patterns, you'll find they accommodate a broad range of techniques.

Tip: It's beneficial to practice visualizing the location of the root notes in each scale position. This provides a reference point on the guitar neck. For example, say you wanted to play a melodic idea on a particular part of the fretboard. It's more intuitive knowing the scale position attached to the root notes in that area than counting from the 1st position to find the right shape.

The Bigger Picture

Our starting point has been to visualize the isolated scale positions found across the guitar neck. However, if our goal is to freely navigate the entire fretboard, we'll want to begin visualizing the neck as a whole. We need to view all these pieces as *connected* in order to move effortlessly through each position when playing. In fact, given a little time, it's possible to view the entire fretboard as one extended scale when playing in any key.

Below we have another diagram using the notes of G major. Here it's narrowed down to start at the 1st position (3rd fret) and end at this same position an octave higher (15th fret). Whereas before this might have seemed like a random cross-section of notes, now we can discern the internal structure of this pattern. We do this by pinpointing each of the seven shapes we've learned within the larger framework. Once we can locate each shape, we're able to observe how these patterns are connected. Each position simply begins in between the overlapping patterns on either side:

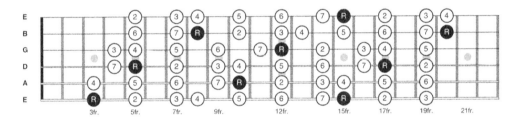

Tip: *Again, it's extremely useful to view the root notes as anchor points within each scale pattern. Locating root notes isn't just about finding our way around; it's also important for structuring melodic ideas. This is especially true when using additional shapes like pentatonic scales or arpeggios within this framework or attempting to play over key changes.*

Ascending & Descending

Now it's time to put our hard work to the test! Here are two fantastic exercises for connecting each section of the larger framework we've been working with. These exercises will assess our success in familiarizing ourselves with each individual position. Here we'll ascend and descend alternately through each pattern until we've come full circle around the guitar neck. Admittedly, this can be difficult at first. Initially, it may be easier to cycle through just two or three shapes at a time until you're able to play these entire exercises in full.

Note: Although each exercise can be played using alternate picking, for maximum speed and fluidity, experiment with the outlined picking technique. These exercises demonstrate a popular *economy* approach to playing three-note-per-string patterns. Here we use consecutive downstrokes when ascending from one string to another and consecutive upstrokes when descending the alternate way.

The first part of this exercise ascends from the 1st position.

Exercise 2.8

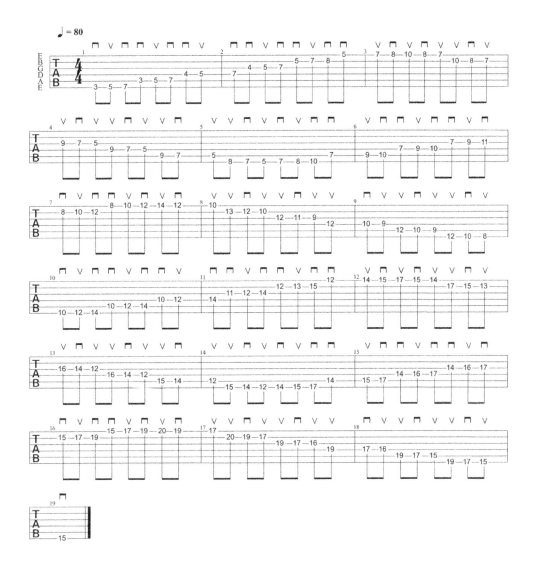

The second part of this exercise descends from the 1st position, one octave higher.

Exercise 2.9

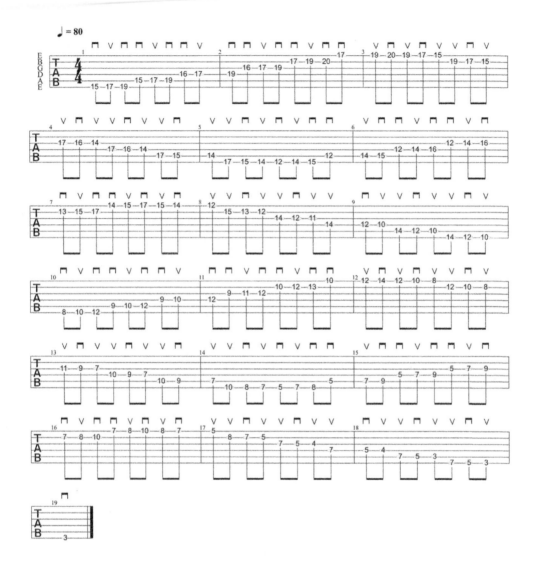

Focus Points

- Learn each of the outlined scale patterns in full. They'll become fundamental for moving forward in this book (and in your wider guitar pursuits). Again, concentrate on each shape separately before moving on to the next position.

- Practice visualizing how each individual pattern overlaps and interconnects with the surrounding shapes. And become familiar with locating the root notes within each scale position.

- Focus on practicing the **Ascending & Descending** exercises outlined. Remember to start slowly and be as accurate as possible, breaking down these exercises to focus initially on smaller sections if necessary.

3

Creative Navigation

Now that we have a solid framework in place, this chapter looks at techniques for working more creatively with these patterns on the fretboard.

Introduction

So far, we've highlighted how the major scale exists as a foundational structure across the entire fretboard. We then discussed isolating and learning the particular positions that make up this larger framework. The task now is making this information more useable in real musical applications. As helpful as scales are, the end goal is always to do something creative and musical with what we've learned. One way to practice this is by introducing more interesting ways of playing these patterns using various scale *sequences*.

In the first chapter, we mentioned that three-note-per-string patterns are compatible with a wide range of playing techniques. Having already introduced the concept of economy picking (in **Chapter 2**), we'll now demonstrate some other popular approaches to experiment with.

Note: For simplicity, all examples will be demonstrated using the 1st position of G major. The main thing isn't the scale shape, but rather the *sequence* being applied to the shape. Each technique will translate to any position we've looked at. You may find it more comfortable to practice these sequences higher on the fretboard. Additionally, the suggested tempo for these exercises is 100 BPM. This is only a guide; it's important to start by practicing each exercise accurately at a comfortable tempo.

Sequence 1 | Alternate Picking (A)

This initial sequence doubles as an exercise in alternate picking. The sequence moves three steps forward, one step back through the scale. Used in small bursts, this concept is a popular way to create more mileage when ascending or descending through smaller note groupings within a scale pattern.

Exercise 3.1

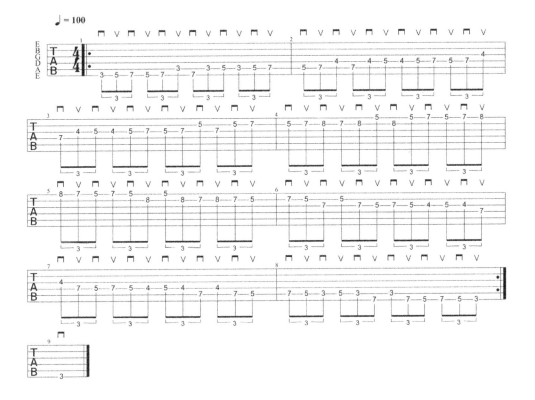

Tip: Building speed in our playing is first and foremost a byproduct of accuracy. One key to playing fast is actually learning to play slowly. Make sure you achieve accuracy and consistency in your technique at slower tempos before trying to increase your speed.

Sequence 2 | Alternate Picking (B)

In this next sequence, we're again practicing our alternate picking. Here we're simply adding repetition to the scale as we move through each string. This is a common technique for extending scale runs and building up picking speed.

Exercise 3.2

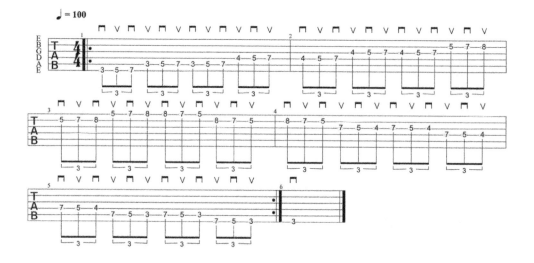

> **Tip:** Many guitarists find smaller, thicker, and sharper guitar picks more conducive to faster playing. Experiment with holding the pick at a 45-degree angle to the strings to help minimize unnecessary movements in your picking action.

Sequence 3 | Legato (A)

In this sequence, we're applying a series of hammer-ons and pull-offs (often referred to as *legato*) to ascend and descend through the scale. Similar to the first exercise in this chapter, we're again moving three steps forward, one step back through the scale. This time, however, each step represents a string instead of a single note. This is a popular technique for building strength and speed in our left hand.

Exercise 3.3

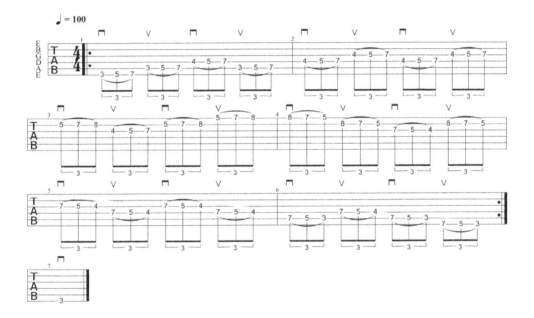

Tip: Here we're only picking the first note of each beat. We're then using our left hand to hammer-on or pull-off the notes following on each string (depending on whether the sequence is ascending or descending). Be sure to keep each note consistent in volume with the initial picked note, letting each one ring clearly for its full duration.

Sequence 4 | Legato (B)

This next pattern again uses a popular legato sequence for developing strength and fluidity in the left hand. In contrast to the previous exercise, this sequence starts with a pull-off. It then moves through a simple repetitive cycle that's looped on each string as we move through the scale.

Exercise 3.4

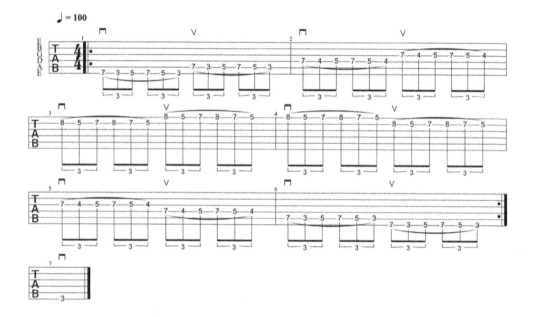

Tip: In addition to consistency in volume, be sure to focus on consistency in timing. Legato should ideally sound like a fluid movement between notes. Developing a smooth, flowing motion in your playing involves cultivating a keen awareness for both dynamics and timing.

Sequence 5 | String Skipping

Next we have a string-skipping sequence, again using this legato technique. Here we're moving through the pattern by missing a string and then doubling back. In addition to mixing up the way we usually play through scales, this sequence will test and train the accuracy of our left hand.

Exercise 3.5

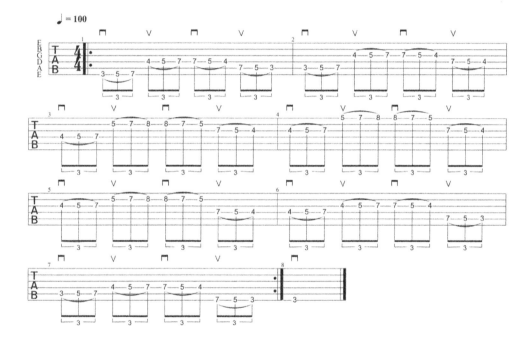

Tip: Accuracy involves playing the correct notes cleanly with clear sustain and no unnecessary string noise. Concentrate on fretting notes with precision, using the tips of your fingers. Avoid lazy, clumsy, or unintentional contact between the strings and your left hand.

Sequence 6 | Odd Note Groupings

This final sequence is an example of how unusual note groupings can add interest to our phrasing. We often think in terms of *even* phrases that consistently land on the same beat. Instead, here we're grouping sections in five-note repetitions using legato as we move through the scale. This technique is a creative way to mix up the more typical melodic groupings we're used to hearing.

Exercise 3.6

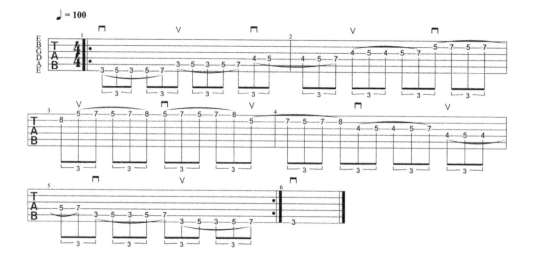

> **Tip:** *Speed isn't just about playing things faster. A great way to experiment with different speeds is by changing the rhythm, not the tempo. Each exercise outlined in this chapter uses triplets (three notes per beat). However, these sequences could also be played using 8th notes (two notes per beat), 16th notes (four notes per beat), or even 16th note triplets (six notes per beat). Try experimenting with the way simple changes in rhythm can completely alter the sound and speed of a pattern.*

A Quick Note on Speed

Unfortunately, developing speed is sometimes emphasized over other aspects of guitar playing that are equally, if not more, important. Consider the importance of a great ear for melody, having solid rhythm, thinking creatively, and being sensitive to feel, dynamics, and emotion in a song. These things will get you much further as a musician than just being able to play something *fast*.

However, since so many guitarists still seem fascinated with speed, there are some essentials to keep in mind. Building speed in your playing is a byproduct of two key things:

- **Accuracy:** As already stated, one key to playing fast is first learning to play slowly. It's important to remember that playing something *fast* isn't the same as playing something *badly at a fast tempo*. Make sure you achieve accuracy and consistency in your technique at slower tempos before trying to increase your speed.

- **Economy:** Ever wondered why fast playing often looks effortless? That's because it often is! Economy is about not expending any more effort than is actually required. Smooth, relaxed movements are far more conducive to faster playing than tense, rigid movements. In addition to keeping as relaxed as possible, we want to focus on minimizing the movements our hands are making (in terms of their distance from the strings). Perhaps it's more helpful to think about speed as the result of smaller, more efficient movements as opposed to just *quicker* ones.

Get Creative

For those wanting to push themselves further, why not combine each sequence in this chapter with the **Ascending & Descending** exercises covered in the previous chapter? Try applying each specific sequence to both exercises. You could even experiment with playing randomly through different sequences each time you ascend or descend an alternate position.

Ultimately, the sequences covered in this chapter represent just a handful of ideas for navigating scale positions more creatively. As always, these are just suggestions to help you think for yourself. Practice mixing up techniques (e.g., using legato on picked sequences and picking on legato sequences), or better yet, come up with new sequences and patterns of your own.

It's important to remember that in real musical situations, we'd hopefully do something more dynamic than just playing scale sequences. However, used in small bursts, sequence ideas can be very handy for moving between different parts of the fretboard. They're also useful for connecting melodic lines and adding flourishes of speed or intensity to your playing. So let your ears guide you and keep experimenting!

Focus Points

- Using the 1st position of the major scale, practice the sequences outlined in this chapter at a slow tempo. Experiment with these sequences in different keys. (They may initially feel more comfortable played higher on the guitar neck.) Try increasing the tempo or moving to faster rhythms when each sequence can be played fluently.

- Once these sequences feel comfortable using the 1st position, try applying them to alternate positions of the major scale. Remember, because each pattern uses three notes per string, all sequences are easily transferable between scale positions.

- Try mixing up sequences with the various techniques demonstrated in this chapter (alternate picking, legato, etc.). Experiment with different rhythms and try to come up with some sequences of your own. Explore how you might use small bursts of these sequence ideas *musically* in your playing.

4

Breaking Boundaries

This chapter discusses techniques for moving outside scale positions and finding new ways to experiment with melodic ideas on the fretboard.

Introduction

In the previous chapters, we became familiar with some fundamental shapes. We established that these patterns provide a framework for successfully finding our way around the fretboard (regardless of the key center). And we experimented with various ways to apply this information more creatively. This alone offers a huge contribution to any guitarist seeking a more extensive understanding of the fretboard. Visualizing these alternate positions of the major scale across the entire fretboard provides a comprehensive map for crafting musical ideas in any position.

Having laid the groundwork, it now becomes important to *break out* of these core patterns that we've learned. This doesn't negate the importance of these shapes in establishing our fundamental framework. Instead, it's a means of further enhancing and exploring the ways we can creatively apply this information.

Let's Get Horizontal

Vertical scale shapes (like the ones we've been working with) make sense for maximizing our reach within a small area on the fretboard. However, they also limit us to playing within a single position. One of the easiest ways to break out of common scale forms is to visualize them *horizontally* across the guitar neck.

Being able to play through scale patterns in this way is immensely beneficial. It assists in navigating alternate positions with ease and opens up new ways of reinterpreting familiar patterns and ideas. Additionally, this approach allows us to cover a lot of ground quickly when playing.

> *Tip: This isn't as complicated as it initially seems. Remember, we already know the formula of a major scale. It's a series of whole steps, except for the half-step movements after the 3rd and 7th notes. Each string just starts from a different point in this sequence (e.g., in the 1st position, the 5th string starts at the 4th degree, and so on). Therefore, on any string, this formula tells us where we are in relation to the next note. In other words, each scale number indicates whether the next note is a whole step or half step away.*

Single-String Exercises

Below is an example of how to practice this idea by isolating one string at a time. In this exercise, we start on the high E string and ascend three notes at a time. Playing 8th notes, we'll move from the 1st position to the octave higher and then back down again.

Remember, each string repeats the simple major scale structure we're already familiar with. Here it's just starting from the 2nd degree of the scale:

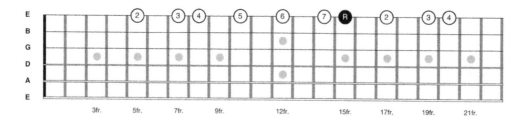

Exercise 4.1

Note: Experiment with this exercise across all six strings. Focus on one string at a time, counting up and back through the scale degrees before moving on to the next string. When you're comfortable with this, try looping through each individual string in order, starting from the 6th string.

Double-String Exercises

Another useful approach for navigating the fretboard horizontally is to practice using multiple sets of strings. In this exercise, we'll ascend and descend in triplets, moving back and forth through each position horizontally, using only the B and E strings.

As you can see, in this example we're focusing on just the 1st and 2nd strings, starting at the 1st position and looping through each subsequent shape:

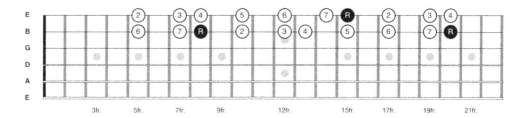

Exercise 4.2

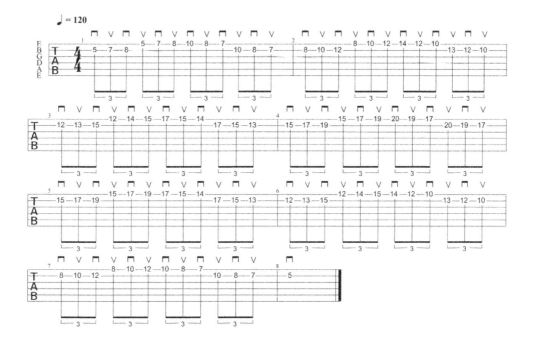

Note: Experiment with shifting this exercise to each set of adjacent strings. Focus on two strings at a time, counting through each scale position as you go. When this feels comfortable, try looping through each set of strings in order, starting from the 5th and 6th strings.

Scales Within Scales

Let's continue this horizontal exploration across the fretboard. In **Chapter 1**, we established that the same idea can be played in multiple ways on the guitar neck. There isn't one particular way to play a certain scale. In fact, because each of the seven positions we've looked at spans multiple octaves, it's possible to isolate numerous single-octave scales within each position. For example, condensing the 1st position of G major to a single octave gives us a smaller shape that repeats throughout the larger framework. The only difference with these shapes is that notes on the first two strings are raised by a half step (because of the guitar's tuning):

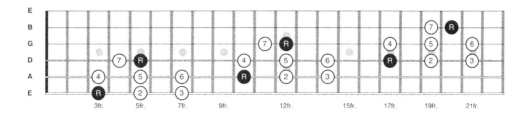

Notice that these aren't really *new* shapes; they're just found within the larger patterns we already know. Having looked at navigating scale positions horizontally using one or two strings, we'll now look at isolating these single-octave shapes across three strings. In this exercise, we'll play back and forth through each single-octave shape on the G, B, and E strings, using 16th notes.

Exercise 4.3

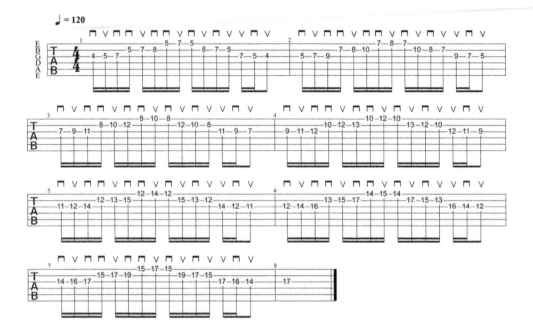

Tip: *Again, try not to look at these as new shapes. We're just isolating smaller positions within the larger framework we've already learned. Focus on the way each position of the major scale can be viewed as a single-octave shape that repeats various times throughout the larger scale shapes.*

Note: Experiment with this exercise using single-octave shapes, starting from the 4th, 5th, and 6th strings. Once this feels natural, play through each single-octave shape in order, starting from the 6th string.

Let's Get Diagonal

Lastly, having explored various approaches to navigating major scale positions horizontally when playing, we can still push this *scales within scales* concept a little further. The example below isolates a single octave of the major scale on the 5th and 6th strings. This basic double-string shape enables us to do something quite interesting. As we'll see, this exact pattern repeats itself diagonally across the fretboard in numerous octaves. Being able to visualize a pattern in this way allows us to shift through various positions, covering an enormous amount of ground quite quickly. This type of diagonal repetition is a popular approach for stringing together blitzing runs up or down the guitar neck:

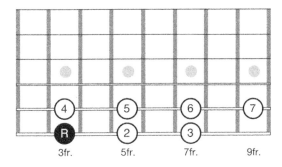

Let's see what this might look like using the 1st position. In this example, we'll use legato to play through each shape repetition in groups of 16th note triplets.

Exercise 4.4

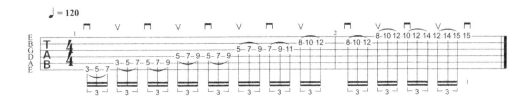

Another popular way to apply this concept is to simplify the scale shape down to just six notes, as demonstrated. In leaving out the 7th note of a pattern, we're left with an even easier shape to repeat across the various octaves. The example shown here uses the 7th position:

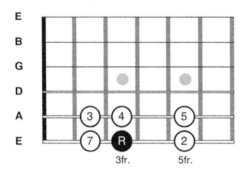

Exercise 4.5

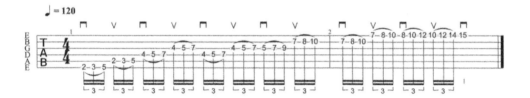

Note: Experiment with both diagonal approaches from each scale position along the 6th string. Try applying various sequences of your own to these repetitive diagonal patterns and explore using the different playing techniques we've covered previously.

Visualization Recap

In this chapter, we've covered four different visualization methods. These help us navigate or break out of the shapes that establish our larger framework. They enhance our ability to use this central framework creatively in a wide range of musical applications. To briefly recap, these methods have focused on:

- **Scale Degrees:** Moving through the scale *degrees* horizontally on each individual string.

- **Scale Positions:** Navigating through the scale *positions* horizontally by limiting ourselves to just two strings.

- **Octave Shapes:** Isolating the single-octave scale *shapes* within the larger framework by moving around the guitar neck across three strings.

- **Diagonal Repetitions:** Pinpointing the various scale *repetitions* that occur when navigating the fretboard in a more diagonal fashion.

A familiarity with multiple ways of interpreting the bigger picture into its smaller components is key for mastering the fretboard. The ability to focus on particular sections of the guitar neck while maintaining an awareness of how each section is connected is a *big* step toward thinking like a pro. Ultimately, you're working toward viewing all this information simultaneously. This will enable you to navigate creatively through different methods and techniques in a way that sounds uninhibited and musical.

Tip: Often, limiting ourselves to particular strings or sections of the fretboard can be helpful creatively. This is because we force ourselves to look at things from a different perspective. Always experiment with playing the same thing in different ways. Not only will this consolidate your knowledge of the fretboard, but you also just might discover something new in the process!

Focus Points

- Work on the exercises in this chapter. Remember, speed isn't the goal just yet. Play at tempos you find comfortable and ensure you aren't making mistakes in attempting to rush through each exercise.

- Practice applying the concepts outlined in this chapter to alternate strings and positions on the guitar. Try to view each note being played in the context of the larger framework. Understand that these horizontal and diagonal patterns aren't *new* sequences to learn; they're just different ways of viewing the patterns we already know.

- Think about the various visualization methods highlighted in each exercise. Experiment with how you might use these alternate ways of visualizing scale patterns creatively in your own playing.

5

Constructing Chords

Now let's shift focus slightly and look at some foundational concepts in music theory relating to the framework we've established.

Introduction

Until now, the bulk of information covered in this book has been tailored largely to the practical. That is, our introduction to the modes has explored what they look like in various shapes and forms, how this framework is foundational to fretboard navigation, and how we can start working creatively with this information. Now that we've established a comprehensive fretboard map, the task is to build our understanding around this central framework.

Understanding the major scale and its various positions provides an extensive structure for navigating the guitar neck in any key. However, as we'll see, this framework also has a wider *theoretical* application. This structure enables us to understand how chords are built and how chord progressions relate to certain keys. It's difficult to fully appreciate how to craft melodic ideas in a song without some understanding of the way chords work. As such, a basic understanding of chord theory is fundamental for both rhythm and lead playing alike.

Stacking Intervals

When we talk about playing in a particular major key (or playing *diatonically*), we mean that notes used to construct chords and melodies come from the same major scale. There's actually a wide range of sonic diversity in the chords we can construct, starting from the different degrees of a major scale. This is done by stacking multiple intervals on top of one another, using the major scale positions as our reference. The simplest form of these chords is built from stacking notes on top of each other in groups of three. This is how basic major, minor, and diminished chords (also known as *triads*) are created.

This process uses the 1st note of a scale position as the chord's starting root note. Since notes too close to one another often sound tense or dissonant when played together, these are avoided in basic chords. This means only notes greater than a whole step apart are used in standard triads. In other words, we pick our starting root note, leapfrog the 2nd note in the scale, stack the 3rd note on the root, skip the 4th, and then stack the 5th on top.

Looking at a single octave of the 1st position (the Ionian mode), this leaves us with the three notes of a major chord. If we play these notes together, reordering them to make things easy on our fingers, we get the familiar E barre chord shape. From the 3rd fret, this gives us a G chord:

I

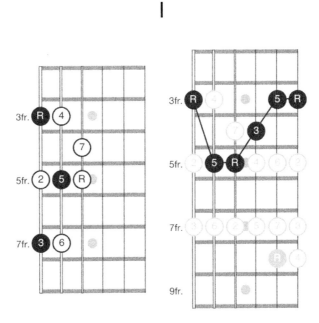

Now we can repeat this process to find the second chord of a major scale, built from the 2nd degree:

ii

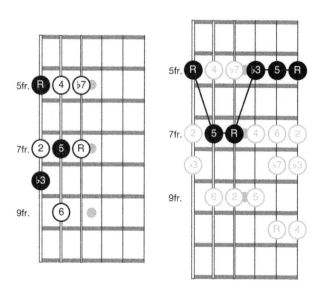

When stacking the 1st, 3rd, and 5th notes from the 2nd position (the Dorian mode) in a way that's practical to play, we get a common Em barre chord shape. Built from the 2nd note of G major, this gives us an Am chord.

Note: As opposed to the 1st mode of the major scale, here we have a flat 3rd. This indicates the note is a half step closer to the root note. You can hear that this flattened 3rd is what gives the chord its *minor* tonality.

Applying this same method to the next position (the Phrygian mode), we see the third chord of a major scale is another minor chord. Built from the 3rd degree in the key of G, this gives us a Bm chord:

iii

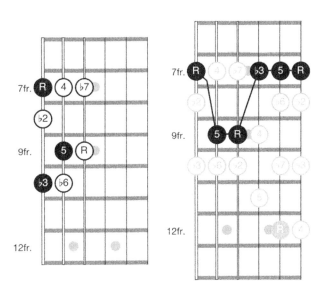

Below we see that the basic triad constructed from the fourth note of a major scale is another major chord. Using notes from the 4th position (the Lydian mode) in the key of G major, we get a C chord:

IV

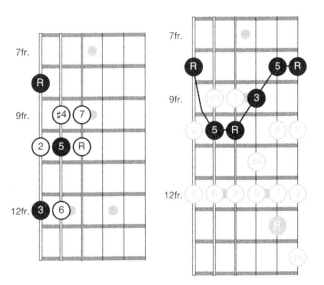

Next, we see that the fifth chord constructed from the 5th position of the major scale (the Mixolydian mode) is another major triad. In this case, a D chord:

V

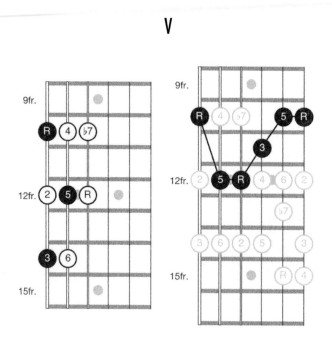

From the 6th position of a major scale (the Aeolian mode), we can stack intervals to build a minor chord. Based on the 6th degree of G major, this would be an Em chord:

vi

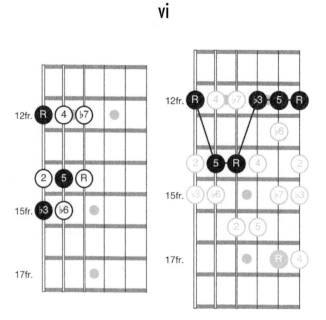

Lastly, through stacking intervals from the 7th position (the Locrian mode), we construct a diminished chord. From the 7th degree of G major, this gives us an F#dim chord:

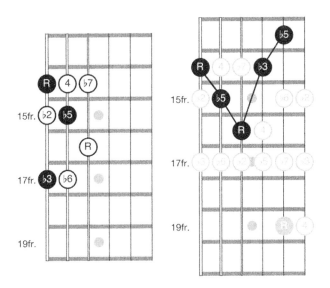

Note: Like a minor chord, a diminished triad is built using a flat 3rd. Unlike a minor chord, however, a diminished chord also includes a flattened 5th, giving its unique *dissonant* sound.

Numbering Chords

There's a tremendous amount of information contained within the seven notes of a major scale. Not only can we construct seven different positions from this scale, but these positions also give us seven different chords corresponding to each degree. While there are various chords here, they all use notes from the same major scale. This explains how we can recognize the key of a song by the chords being used. It also demonstrates how we can build chord progressions of our own in different keys.

It's common to attribute numbers to each chord of the major scale in the same way we'd number each scale degree. As demonstrated in this chapter, we often see chords referenced using Roman numerals relative to each chord position. Typically, uppercase numerals represent major chords, while lowercase numerals symbolize minor chords. Diminished chords are often denoted with an additional symbol (e.g., vii°).

Subsequently, a I - IV - V progression in the key of G major would refer to chords built from the 1st, 4th, and 5th positions of the G major scale. This means our progression would be G - C - D.

> *Tip:* Can a chord belong to more than one key center? Absolutely! As demonstrated, major scales include three major chords and three minor chords. Therefore, it makes sense that any major or minor chord must belong to three different major scales. C, for example, is the I chord of C major, the IV chord of G major, and the V chord of F major. As your playing advances, it's very beneficial to know how the chords in one key relate to other key centers.

Extending Chords

At this point it would be appropriate to briefly reference the topic of chord *embellishments*. So far, we've created basic chord forms by stacking the 1st, 3rd, and 5th intervals from each position (or mode) of the major scale. We've also established that notes stacked too close together often sound tense or dissonant. However, this doesn't mean these other notes are never used. On the contrary, additional notes are commonly used in chords *because* of their harmonic complexity.

In fact, placing closely related notes in separate octaves can dramatically enhance the sophistication or richness of a chord. A common example is when a 7th is used to embellish a basic triad. If we continued stacking scale tones to include this interval, our original G chord would become a Gmaj7 chord. Even though the 7th and root are only a half step apart, they sound quite harmonious when played in different octaves:

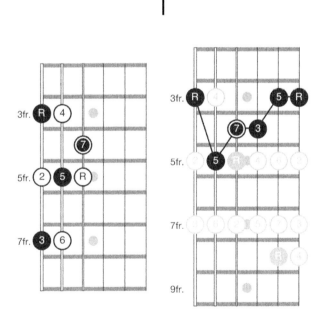

The important thing, if our intention is to stay diatonic (within one key center), is that chord extensions must correspond to their respective scale positions. For example, as already established, like the I chord, the V chord of a major scale is also a major chord. However, their sevenths would be different, because the scale built off of the 5th degree is different from the scale built off of the 1st degree. In other words, looking at both positions, we see that the Mixolydian mode has a flattened 7th, whereas the Ionian mode does not. Therefore, this flat 7th (built from the 5th degree of G major) would turn our D chord into a D7. The difference being that this is a *dominant* chord, as opposed to a major seventh chord:

V

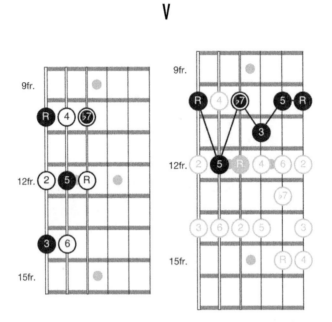

Tip: Experiment with playing each chord from the same root note. Notice how a seemingly small shift in the structure of a chord can dramatically alter the chord's tonal character.

Using Chords

Now that we've established how to build chords using the modal framework, we can explore how this information relates to playing situations. Defining the chords belonging to a particular major scale provides a starting point from which we can create progressions for improvisation and songwriting. As we've covered, each degree of a major scale can be used to build not only a different scale position, but also a different chord. Before creating some progressions to work with, let's review the basic chords in G major. For simplicity, this time we'll voice each shape around the open position.

Exercise 5.1

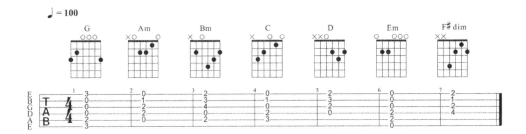

Tip: Although the chords themselves change between keys, the chord formulas do not. For example, the I, IV, and V chords of a major scale will always be major, while the ii, iii, and vi chords will always be minor. Understanding this makes it relatively easy to transcribe chord progressions between different keys.

Tonal Gravity

Having highlighted the basic chords we have to work with, what's next? At this point it makes sense to briefly introduce a concept we'll call *tonal gravity*. This affects our approach to constructing both rhythm and lead ideas. The basic notion is that both chords and melodic ideas have an inherent way of telling us where they want to go. It's like a sense of gravity pulling us one way or another. For example, play a major scale, but this time leave it hanging on the 7th without resolving to the root.

Exercise 5.2

This just doesn't feel right, does it? The whole scale is pulling toward the root note. It feels incomplete left hanging without resolution. Chord progressions function in a similar way, often needing to resolve themselves by moving back to home base, which is the root (or *tonic*) chord.

> **Tip:** As another example, try playing a diminished chord by itself. Again, you'll notice it doesn't feel stable; it's just crying out for resolution!

This concept reflects the important dynamic of *tension* and *release* as central to any creative vocabulary. Being attentive to where a progression or melodic phrase is gravitating toward gives context to our musical ideas. This works both ways, of course. Intentionally *not* taking something where you might expect can be equally as powerful as taking a progression or melody where it feels it needs to go.

Building Progressions

Thus far, we've established the basic chords available in the key we're working with. We then isolated some popular chord shapes to use. Now let's look at an example of a progression that demonstrates these chords together.

Exercise 5.3

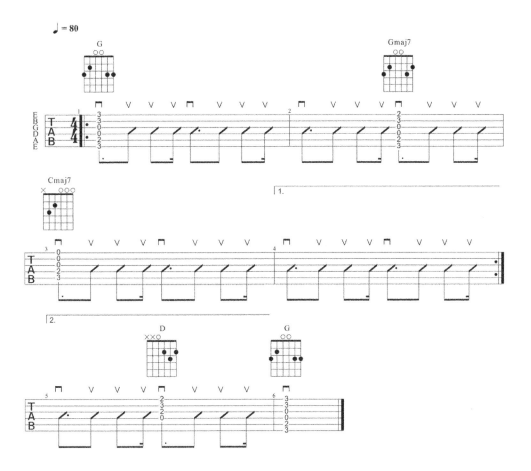

What do we notice about this progression?

- Looking at these chords, we see that the progression uses the I, IV, and V chords of G major. This G major tonality is reinforced by the progression's constant pull back to the G chord.

- The first part of this progression moves between the I and IV chords (G and C). These chords have been embellished with their respective sevenths, adding more color to the progression.

- The last part of this progression moves to the V chord (D) as a turnaround, leading us nicely back to home base at the G chord.

Note: While there aren't strict *rules* for structuring progressions, you'll often see V chords function in this way (leading to the I chord). This is especially true when they're played as dominant seventh chords.

This example prompts the next logical question: Do progressions always have to resolve to the I chord in a major key? The short answer is *no*. Building a progression around the tonic chord of a major key will emphasize the major tonality of the progression. However, this may not always be our intention. For example, let's look at another chord progression.

Exercise 5.4

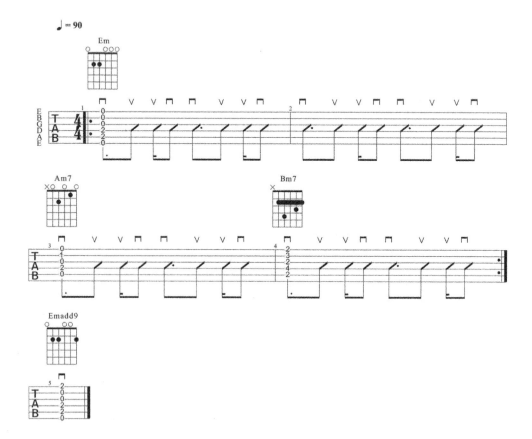

What do we notice about this progression?

- First, the chords being used are the ii, iii, and vi chords of G major. Interestingly, though, there's actually no G major chord here at all! Instead, the progression gravitates towards the Em chord, completely changing the tonal character of this progression.

- Again, there are a few chord embellishments. This progression uses minor seventh extensions for the ii and iii chords (Am7 and Bm7) and also adds a 9th to the final chord for interest. This indicates that chords are often extended past their sevenths (by stacking scale intervals, as illustrated earlier).

- Finally, even though this progression sounds distinctly minor, we're still only using chords from G major. As such, our major scale framework is still relevant, despite this being a minor progression!

From these examples, another question arises: Do chord progressions have to stay diatonic? Not at all! Listen to a few jazz standards and you'll hear how easily progressions can move through different key centers. Even in more mainstream music, it's common for progressions to temporarily *borrow* chords from another key or modulate to a different key center entirely. As you progress beyond this book, one important function of modes will be their usefulness in navigating through key changes. While popular music is often based around a single key center, there's no reason your progressions (or even your improvising) have to stay diatonic. The only real defining factor is, does it sound good to you?

> *Tip:* *Knowing how chords relate to key centers, we can apply this method in reverse to work out how keys relate to chord progressions. For example (assuming a progression is diatonic), any two minor chords separated by a whole step must be the ii and iii chords of the key, because this is the only position where minor chords occur back to back. This is true for major chords as well. The only time they're next to each other in sequence is as the IV and V chords of a key. All we need to do is count back to find our key center.*

Just a Minor Detour

Before moving forward, let's back up a little bit. We've just built a chord progression in the key of Em using the G major scale. How does that work? The answer, as hinted at, is that each major key also has a minor key that it directly relates to. You may have heard this concept referred to as the *relative* minor. In **Chapter 2**, we explained that the mode built from the 6th degree of a major scale is known as the *natural minor* scale. While the notes in both scales are the same, the sound changes depending on the notes being emphasized (another good example of tonal gravity).

In other words, by learning the G major scale framework we've also (without necessarily knowing it) learned the E minor scale framework. Therefore, we don't need to learn the minor scale and all of its positions, because we already know it! This information relates to any major or minor key center. The patterns are all the same; we're just shifting our starting point to different places on the fretboard.

How would we find the patterns in A minor, for example? Well, knowing that A minor is built from the 6th degree, it's easy to find the parent major scale! If we simply count up two positions, we'll find the major scale we're playing relative to. In this case, the scale shapes for A minor are the same as C major. This would also be true for D minor as it relates to F major, C# minor as it relates to E major, F# minor as it relates to A major, and so on.

Focus Points

- Closely revisit the information in this chapter. Become familiar with the way chords are built from positions of the major scale by stacking intervals. Experiment with applying this method to construct chords in alternate keys of your choosing.

- Using the chords in G major, try to work out several ways of playing each chord on the fretboard. Additionally, challenge yourself to work out the 7th extensions for each chord in the scale. (Again, through the process of stacking intervals from each scale position.)

- Try creating a few progressions of your own using the chords in G major. Don't be afraid to embellish chords with extended sevenths where desired. See if you can transpose your progressions (and the two provided) into different keys. Experiment with playing over these progressions as an introduction to navigating the fretboard in various key centers. Remember, the notes and positions will change, but the shapes will not.

6

Hidden Chords & Scales

In this chapter, we'll explore some important concepts for structuring melodic ideas and working with the patterns and techniques we've learned.

Introduction

Thus far, this book has been structured step-by-step to help you develop a comprehensive map for fretboard navigation and improvisation. Beyond this, we've touched on various related techniques and key theoretical aspects. The intention has been to provide the appropriate tools for understanding and experimenting with this information.

The bulk of this content has focused on developing a practical command of the fretboard in our approach to lead playing. At this point, it's important to discuss some key ideas invaluable for working with this information in real-life musical contexts. As stated at the beginning of this book, the focus isn't solely on what we play, but also our *approach* to what we play. The most immediate breakthroughs in our playing often come from adjustments to how we *think* as guitar players. In this chapter, we'll explore essential concepts for cultivating musicality within our melodic ideas.

Strong Notes

It seems appropriate at this juncture to revisit the concept of tonal gravity. If you attempted to improvise over the progressions in the previous chapter, you'll have noticed something quite interesting. Although the notes on the fretboard stayed the same, they sounded different when the tonal context changed. In the first example, the progression pulled toward the sound of G major. In the second example, the progression pulled toward the sound of E minor. This is a fundamental point when thinking about melodic phrasing. Not all notes are created equal in terms of their *tonal* weight. Some notes create tension against the chords they're played over, pulling us one way or another, while other notes feel stable, strong, and resolved. We need both.

Logically, if the chords feel like they're pulling toward a tonal center, it makes sense that the notes played over those chords would feel the same. Typically, we'll find that tones contained within our tonic chord are the stronger notes, because they emphasize the momentum of the progression. This doesn't mean we should only play notes found in a G chord over a G major progression. It simply suggests that these tones typically establish a stronger sense of tonal gravity within the larger scale framework. A popular application of this idea is where a melodic phrase begins on and/or resolves to a note of the tonic chord.

Example 6.1

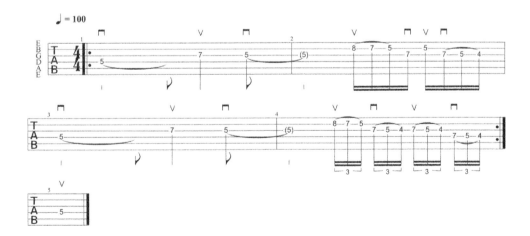

Hidden Chord Shapes

A practical way to visualize the concept of strong notes is to highlight the basic chord shapes found within each position of the major scale. In the example below, we've isolated the G major chord tones (G, B, and D) within the larger framework. These chord tones are derived from stacking intervals, as discussed in **Chapter 5**. A good analogy when creating melodic ideas is to view these notes as central *branches*, providing stability and structure. In turn, the other notes can be thought of as *leaves*, adding color and interest to the tonal palette:

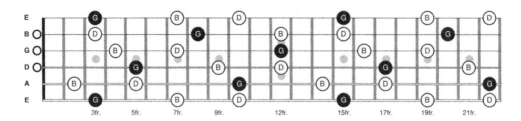

This may seem like a lot of information to memorize. However, looking closer we find that this seemingly random collection of notes actually comprises five basic chord shapes. Most of us are probably very familiar with these shapes, since C, A, G, E, and D are often the first chords guitar players learn:

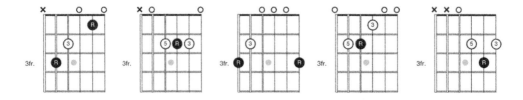

Within the larger framework, these basic chord shapes connect in sequence across the guitar neck. They're built from the G root notes on the bottom three strings throughout the various scale positions.

> *Tip: This concept is often referred to as the CAGED system. Notice that each shape cycles consistently in the C - A - G - E - D sequence moving up the fretboard.*

Major Chord Shapes

Let's take a closer look at these five major chord shapes and how they relate to each position we've been working with. We can see below that every chord shape overlaps one or more major scale position as demonstrated.

1ˢᵗ & 7ᵗʰ Positions | E Shape

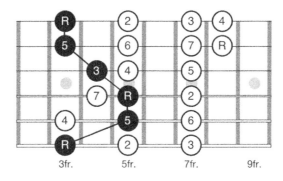

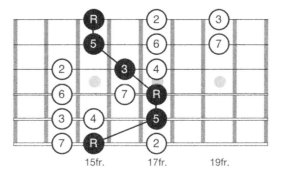

2ⁿᵈ Position | D Shape

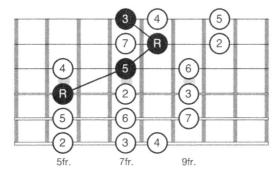

3rd Position | C Shape

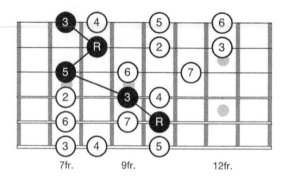

7fr.   9fr.   12fr.

4th & 5th Positions | A Shape

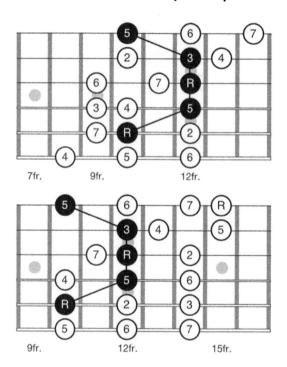

7fr.   9fr.   12fr.

9fr.   12fr.   15fr.

6th Position | G Shape

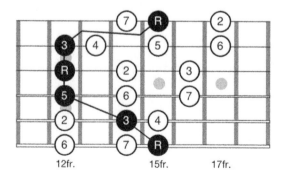

12fr.   15fr.   17fr.

The concept of visualizing chord tones has numerous uses within this framework. For example, we can mirror this same approach with the relative minor scale. Although the overall framework stays the same, we can shift the tonal gravity in the scale to emphasize the sound of E minor. In other words, the chord tones in Em (E, G, and B) now become the *strong* notes we can target in our melodic phrasing. Again, these chord shapes are mapped in sequence across the guitar neck, extending from the E root notes on the bottom three strings:

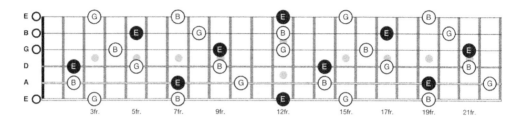

Tip: *In a minor key, these shapes still follow the C - A - G - E - D sequence. The difference is that each chord is a minor shape instead of a major one. Take note, in either situation both major and minor variations of the same chord shape coincide with the same relative scale position.*

Minor Chord Shapes

The following examples demonstrate the way each minor chord shape relates to the various minor scale positions. Notice that when improvising over a minor progression, the natural minor scale (built from the 6th degree of its parent major scale) now becomes our 1st position, or starting point. Put simply, we're shifting the tonal gravity so that E is now the root note of the scale. In turn, this requires switching the visual reference point within each position (from G to E).

Remember, the framework itself doesn't change; we're only adjusting the notes we want to emphasize. To reiterate, even though the scale patterns shift position, the same basic chord types (in their minor form) overlap the same relative positions of the minor scale.

1st & 7th Positions | Em Shape

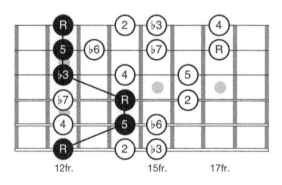

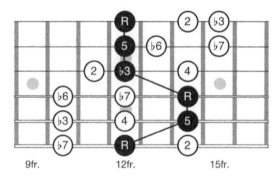

2ⁿᵈ Position | Dm Shape

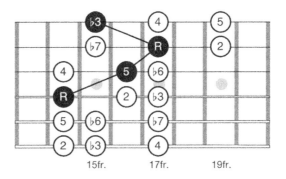

3ʳᵈ Position | Cm Shape

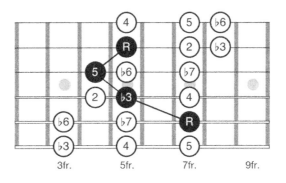

4ᵗʰ & 5ᵗʰ Positions | Am Shape

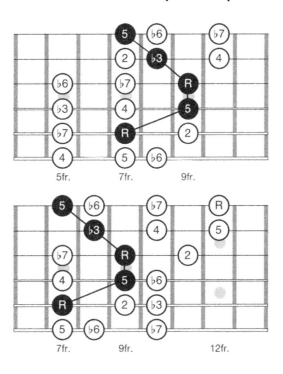

6th Position | Gm Shape

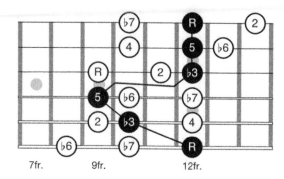

7fr.   9fr.   12fr.

These previous sections demonstrate how to visualize the chord tones, or *strong* notes contained within the larger major/minor scale framework. As we've seen, it's common for a progression to pull toward the major sound of the I chord (major scale) or the minor sound of the vi chord (minor scale). However, we must remember that major scales contain chords from every scale degree. Progressions can also be structured to revolve around other chords in the scale, such as the ii chord or the V chord. This would alter the chord tones we may want to highlight or base our melodic ideas around.

Some guitar players even prefer targeting specific chord tones coinciding with every single chord change in a progression. This is especially handy if a progression moves through various key centers. Often referred to as *playing over the changes,* this approach is extremely common in jazz, among other genres.

Tip: Don't be overwhelmed by this seeming information overload! The point is that there are various ways to apply the information contained within the major scale and its modes. Put simply, the tonal character of the notes you play will change depending on the progression you're playing over. Just remember to let your ears guide you to the notes and phrases that sound most musically appropriate in any situation.

Hidden Pentatonic Shapes

The concept of chord tones having greater tonal weight than other notes is why many use *arpeggios* extensively in guitar playing. (This involves playing, or *sweep picking*, through the notes of a chord in sequence.) Arpeggios are a great way to target specific chord tones in soloing and composition. However, there's another extremely useful way to highlight tonal gravity within the scale framework we've established. This brings us to a discussion of the ever-popular *pentatonic* scale.

Many of us will be familiar with the pentatonic scale. It has become an absolute staple in rock, blues, and country playing. This is one of the first scales we're generally introduced to when we start attempting to solo. What some may not realize is that a pentatonic scale is essentially a major scale, just with a few notes missing. In other words, within the major scale we find the pentatonic scale hiding.

As we know, in a major scale there are four notes separated by just a half step. Melodically, the 4th tends to pull down to the 3rd, and the 7th tends to pull up to the root. In a major pentatonic scale, however, these half steps are removed. As such, this tension between notes is avoided, giving the scale a more open sound. Furthermore, without the 4th and 7th, three of the five remaining notes are chord tones (the root, 3rd, and 5th):

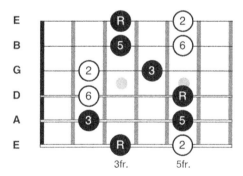

This emphasis on strong notes is even more evident when comparing the E minor scale with the E minor pentatonic scale. Similarly, the minor pentatonic is a five-note scale that omits the half-step movements found in the natural minor scale. Here the remaining notes resemble the exact intervals we find in an Em7 chord (with the exception of the 4th degree). Again, three of the five notes in this scale are chord tones from the Em triad. Additionally, we're also left with the flat 7th, which holds a similar tonal weight because it's such a common minor chord extension:

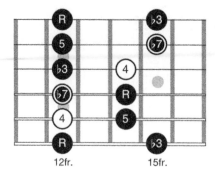

12fr.   15fr.

Don't worry if this little exercise in theory seems a touch confusing. The main takeaway is that pentatonic scales are full of strong, resolved-sounding notes. That's a big part of why they're so popular; they work extremely well in so many contexts. However, this is also part of the problem we encounter when relying solely on pentatonic scales. We end up limiting the colors available within our tonal palette. Our licks and ideas have a tendency to sound a lot more conventional or predictable given that they're so widely popularized. This isn't necessarily a bad thing, but it can leave some guitarists wanting a little more interest and nuance in their playing. This involves breaking out of these common pentatonic *box* shapes when desired.

The Hybrid Approach

One main idea being outlined here is that pentatonic scales use notes common to their parent major and minor scales. We've already established that major scale shapes can also be viewed as positions of the natural minor scale. Therefore, logically, both major and minor pentatonic scales are already contained within the larger framework we've established.

Below are the five pentatonic scale positions, one or more of which you'll hopefully find familiar. In the key of G major, we'd consider the initial shape on the left our 1st position. The other shapes can be viewed as inversions of this scale. They contain the same notes but start from different points along the low E string. (A concept you should be accustomed to by now.) It hopefully comes as no surprise that each shape can also be used as positions of the E minor pentatonic scale. In this context, the final shape on the right would be considered our 1st position, because it's built from the E root note:

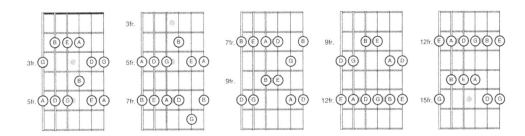

Given their popularity, it's a fair assumption that most guitar players have spent a lot of time playing licks and ideas based around these patterns. Using a modal framework doesn't mean discarding these hours spent. The key concept here is simple: Because these patterns are contained within the larger scale framework, there's no need for an either/or approach. Why not use both? Why not keep using these pentatonic patterns and just embellish them with other colors and tones from the wider major scale framework? Not only is this a more creative way to view pentatonic scales, but it also represents a very musical way to craft our lead ideas.

Tip: This approach makes a lot of sense when we understand that pentatonic scales include mostly tonic chord tones. And, as already established, these are generally considered our strongest and most resolved-sounding notes.

Major Shapes

As you'll see in the following patterns, we can demonstrate what this *hybrid* scale concept might look like on the fretboard. We're simply picking up the closest notes from the larger framework in direct proximity to each original pentatonic pattern. A more technical way of saying this is that we're adding the 4th and 7th as optional notes to embellish the major pentatonic shapes. And we're adding the 2nd and 6th as optional notes to embellish the minor pentatonic shapes. While they represent different scale degrees, in both the major or minor contexts these patterns are the same.

First, let's look at embellishing each major pentatonic shape with additional notes from the surrounding major scale positions. Notice that the circled intervals represent the chord shapes we've already looked at and how they overlap these patterns.

Note: While the light gray notes are part of each major scale shape, we'll exclude them from these patterns for simplicity.

Pentatonic Shape 1 | Scale Position 7 | E Shape

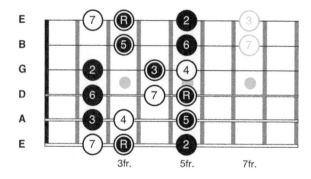

Pentatonic Shape 2 | Scale Position 1 | D Shape

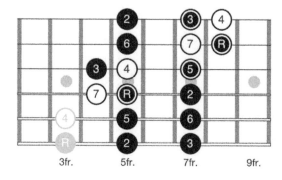

Pentatonic Shape 3 | Scale Position 3 | C Shape

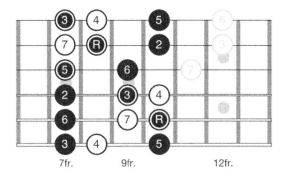

Pentatonic Shape 4 | Scale Position 4 | A Shape

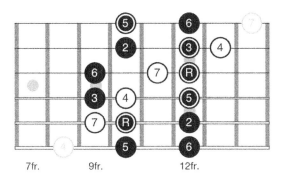

Pentatonic Shape 5 | Scale Position 6 | G Shape

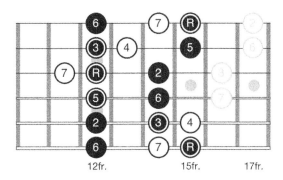

Minor Shapes

Now let's turn our attention to how the minor pentatonic shapes relate to the wider framework. Again, take note of the chord shape outlined within each pattern. Remember, these patterns are the same as those in the previous section; we're just using the minor scale as our starting point by shifting the root notes.

Pentatonic Shape 1 | Scale Position 1 | Em Shape

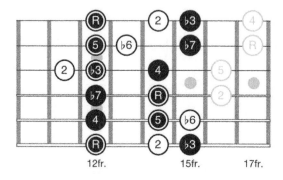

Pentatonic Shape 2 | Scale Position 2 | Dm Shape

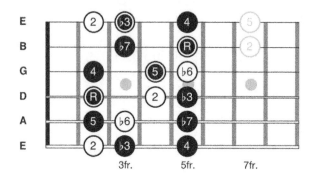

Pentatonic Shape 3 | Scale Position 3 | Cm Shape

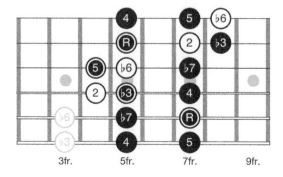

Pentatonic Shape 4 | Scale Position 5 | Am Shape

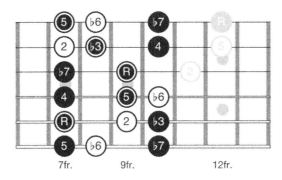

7fr.   9fr.   12fr.

Pentatonic Shape 5 | Scale Position 6 | Gm Shape

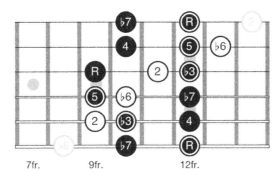

7fr.   9fr.   12fr.

Note: Unlike the previous major patterns, the number alongside each shape and position now refer to minor patterns.

Tip: Like the different chords we find within the major scale, there's also more than one pentatonic scale hidden within this framework. We've viewed pentatonic shapes in relation to their parent major and minor scales. This is how they're commonly used. However, we could also build additional pentatonic scales corresponding to other major and minor chords in the key. For example, in the key of G, the IV and ii chords share the same major/minor pentatonic shapes (C and Am). This is also true for the V and iii chords (D and Bm). Admittedly, these additional pentatonic scales won't always give the desired sound, though it's interesting to experiment with them alongside the core shapes we've focused on.

Visualizing Shapes

As you learn and experiment with each pattern in this chapter, it may be helpful to consider a few final things. There are multiple ways of visualizing these overlapping shapes when improvising or songwriting. Ultimately, this depends on your preferred reference point:

- **Pentatonic Scales:** Perhaps the most popular method is the one outlined in the previous few sections, being mindful of the way chord tones and additional surrounding notes relate to the pentatonic shapes you may already know.

- **Modal Patterns:** Additionally, like the approach of this book, you may prefer to use the modal shapes as your starting point, viewing the various chord shapes and pentatonic patterns as smaller structures contained within this larger framework.

- **CAGED Shapes:** Lastly, you might like to use the five basic CAGED shapes as your key reference point, visually connecting the closest overlapping pentatonic and modal patterns to each individual chord shape on the fretboard.

Essentially, these are just different ways of visualizing the same information. No approach is better than any other, but it's helpful to know which one makes most sense to you. In any case, as repeatedly emphasized, understanding where the root notes overlap in any pattern or position will be extremely useful. Root notes are the common thread between all these approaches.

Finally, if this theoretical exploration into different ways of targeting chord tones and scale shapes has left you overwhelmed, fear not! If you remember nothing else, at the end of the day it's always about using your ears. Developing a theoretical understanding of how things work undoubtedly aids creativity, but it's never a substitute for it. Always favor what you think sounds best over what you assume is more *theoretically* correct. The more you experiment with different ideas, the clearer things become. After all, you can't talk about playing guitar without using the word *play*.

Focus Points

- Practice moving through the positions of the major scale and focus on the chord shapes found within each position, as outlined in this chapter. Do this in both major and minor keys and experiment with how targeting these notes might influence your melodic ideas.

- Experiment using pentatonic scales within the larger framework. Practice playing the five pentatonic shapes using notes from the parent major/minor scale positions to embellish each pattern. Remember, these *hybrid* shapes are the same in both major and minor keys. Practice visualizing how the modes, pentatonic scales, and CAGED shapes overlap and interconnect with one another.

- Listen closely to a collection of songs you find particularly memorable or emotive (preferably from artists in different genres). Reflect on the concepts covered in the last few chapters. Think about tonal gravity and the way melodic phrases interact with the movement of chords. Consider the note choice, use of melody, and phrasing. What specific things do you notice? What elements make these melodic ideas sound engaging? In light of the ideas discussed, how might you apply these concepts to your own playing?

7

Motion & Emotion

This final chapter looks at important exercises for practicing and consolidating the various concepts and techniques we've covered.

Introduction

By now we've worked on getting our entire fretboard framework thoroughly in place. We explored the way this *blueprint* can shift to function in any key, not only for improvisation or composition, but also for building chords and understanding chord progressions. We talked about the concept of tonal gravity and highlighted different ways to view the information contained within this larger framework.

In this final section, we depart from the theoretical exploration of the last couple of chapters. We'll turn our attention back to the task of experimenting with this information on the guitar neck. This chapter revisits many of the concepts and techniques we've covered by introducing two fundamental exercises. These exercises are extremely effective for putting things into perspective on the fretboard.

Melodic Motion

For this first exercise, let's take the G major chord progression from **Chapter 5** and apply some improvised melodic movement over the top. Note that our key focus is on *motion*. While dynamics and expression are a huge part of crafting melodic ideas, these aren't the goal of this exercise. Here are the guidelines we'll be working with:

- This exercise is all about melodic movement; we're *not* trying to solo.

- Listening to the backing track, start slowly with quarter notes (one note per beat) and begin moving around the fretboard in the key of G. Try to do this without stopping or skipping a beat.

- Try not to stay in one place for too long. The goal is to keep moving, covering as much fretboard real estate as possible.

- While maintaining a quarter-note rhythm, try to mix 'n' match among various exercises covered in this book (e.g., moving through two-octave shapes, into single-string patterns, into one-octave shapes, into double-string patterns, into diagonal shapes, etc.). Think about alternating techniques and sequences, switching between alternate picking, legato, economy picking, string skipping, and so on.

- As you move around the fretboard in a consistent and steady fashion, think about the concept of tonal gravity. Pay attention to notes that feel resolved and those that add tension. Experiment with outlining the different chord tones and pentatonic patterns you can see. Challenge yourself to play separately through each modal position, followed by the relative pentatonic shape and then the overlapping chord tones.

- Once you feel fluent with this, try increasing the speed of the exercise using 8th notes (two notes per beat). Additionally, you can move to triplets (three notes per beat) and then 16th notes (four notes per beat) as it seems appropriate.

Note: Want more jam tracks? Be sure to check out *5-Minute Guitar Jams* as a supplementary practice guide. This book features an album of high-quality backing tracks to accompany your practice.

Melodic Emotion

The last exercise in motion is fantastic for creatively and intuitively honing our skills at fretboard navigation. However, the end goal is always about taking what we've learned and doing something musical with it. Concentrated meandering around the fretboard (as illustrated in the previous exercise) is a great practice technique, but it should never be our approach for constructing solos or melodic phrases.

For this exercise, let's use the second chord progression in **Chapter 5** and take an alternate approach to playing over it. If the first exercise was about consistent movement, covering as much space as possible, this next exercise is about exactly the opposite. Now we want to limit ourselves by focusing solely on *feel* and *dynamics*. These are the guidelines for this exercise:

- Listening to the backing track, try forgetting all the exercises we've practiced up to now. Concentrate on a single position on the fretboard, preferably staying within one octave.

- It's important to begin this exercise with only two or three notes. Sometimes limiting what we play forces us to be more creative with how we play. Use your ears and experiment with creating simple melodic phrases or *hooks*. Try hearing the melody you want to play in your head before playing it on the fretboard.

- Avoid unnecessarily noodling around on the fretboard. This is an exercise in self-imposed moderation.

- Focus on dynamics, feel, and expression. Practice targeting strong notes. Think about phrasing, use of rhythm, and space. Sometimes what you *don't* play says just as much as what you do. You only have a few notes to use, so don't waste them!

- Draw on every tool you can think of to make these notes work for you. Try experimenting with popular playing techniques like bends, slides, or vibrato. See if you can create something interesting, memorable, and emotive against the backing track.

- Repeat this exercise in multiple positions on the guitar neck. Slowly extend to incorporate more notes as it seems appropriate, but remember, the focus is on feel and melody. Consciously using fewer notes forces us to think creatively about how our melodic phrases are delivered.

Tip: *The goal of fretboard navigation isn't to show off what we know by shredding aimlessly all over the place (despite how fast we can do this!). It's so we're empowered to communicate something musical and engaging. A good starting point for crafting solos lies somewhere between these last two exercises, focusing on melodic and interesting ideas while having the freedom to move fluently through different scale positions.*

Focus Points

- Become familiar with both exercises in **Melodic Motion** and **Melodic Emotion**. These are fantastic practice techniques to revisit regularly, regardless of your skill level. Try switching things around, using the E minor progression to practice fretboard navigation and the G major progression to improvise with short melodic phrases.

- As you work on improvisation (using these or other progressions), be mindful of the chord tones and pentatonic shapes relating to the progressions you're playing over. Practice viewing these shapes as connected to the larger framework we've established. Continue experimenting with how targeting these shapes can influence the sound of your musical phrases and ideas.

- Reflecting on tonal gravity, think about how phrasing, dynamics, and sense of space might complement the notes you play. Experiment using this information to your advantage in creating phrases that sound musical and melodic. Focus on crafting ideas that are interesting and memorable, letting your ears (not your fingers) guide you.

Final Thoughts

Congratulations on completing **Lead Guitar Breakthrough**!

Unlike other content you might find on lead guitar, the intention of this book hasn't been to bombard you with an arsenal of guitar licks. Nor has it been to offer instruction on the best way to play and sound like somebody else. Although these teaching strategies have their place, our focus was on establishing an overarching framework for approaching any style or genre. The goal was to provide the tools for a comprehensive, well-rounded approach to fretboard navigation. We discussed central concepts in improvisation and songwriting and explored key techniques for experimenting with these ideas.

It's my sincere hope that this book has answered many questions and in doing so has raised many more. This book was never intended to do the thinking for you, but to inspire you to think for yourself. As such, when you refer to this resource from time to time, you may just learn something different, understand something better, or see something you missed previously. This isn't because the content has transformed but because, as your learning progresses, *you* are transforming.

One might expect that the more advanced a person's playing becomes, the less they value the fundamentals. In my experience, however, it has been precisely the opposite. The more you learn, the more you understand the importance of the essentials. This resource has sought to provide a solid, practical foundation for overcoming the roadblocks people encounter in their lead playing. Like all good foundations, this content exists to be built on. It's in the process of moving beyond the fundamentals that we discover just how truly valuable they are.

May this book help inspire you toward continued learning and creativity.

LEARN YOUR GUITAR SCALES

Tips & Techniques

MODES, PENTATONICS & ARPEGGIOS EXPLAINED

LUKE ZECCHIN

This book is dedicated to my wonderful parents. Thank you for buying my first guitar, coming to my gigs, and never telling me to get a real job.

Published by **GuitarIQ.com**

Copyedited by Allister Thompson

Proofread by Dan Foster

Illustrated by Jasmin Zecchin

Contents

Preface

Welcome, and thank you for choosing *Learn Your Guitar Scales*.

For many guitar players, learning scales can quickly become overwhelming. In part, this is due to the seemingly endless scale types and alternatives that exist. It can be complex enough memorizing the names of all these scales, let alone what they look like on the fretboard and how to use them! While feeling intimidated is understandable, it isn't necessary. There are numerous languages in the world, but a person doesn't need to know them all to say something worthwhile.

The intention of this book is to focus on the central elements that will have the greatest impact on your playing. These foundational concepts and patterns will enable you to navigate a broad range of playing situations, regardless of style or genre. Mastering the fundamentals is infinitely more beneficial than being overwhelmed by so many options that you end up using none of them effectively.

This highlights a common frustration with many scale books for guitar. Being shown a multitude of scale patterns on the fretboard can be useful, but it provides little explanation regarding how to actually learn, practice, and apply them. What's the point of knowing all this information if we can't make something musical out of it?

In contrast, the focus here isn't simply on demonstrating what different patterns *look* like, but on explaining how they're built, how they relate to one another, and how they're commonly used. Touching on everything from basic concepts to more advanced applications, we'll take a detailed look at the formative scales and arpeggios that shape the essential creative framework for guitar.

I sincerely hope this book provides renewed insight and inspires continued development and innovation in your playing.

—Luke Zecchin

Introduction

In light of the vast amount of existing material on guitar scales, it seems appropriate to start by outlining what this book is *not*. This isn't intended to be a collection of every possible guitar scale you might encounter. While a scale *encyclopedia* like that might occasionally be a helpful reference, in reality a resource of such magnitude is likely to confuse as many guitar players as it helps. More importantly, it's very unlikely most of that information would contribute to your core musical vocabulary on guitar.

Instead, this guide focuses on patterns rooted in the *diatonic* world, or in other words, scales and arpeggios that are derived from the same key center. Why? These diatonic patterns underpin the foundations of all Western music. As such, an extremely wide range of musical situations, spanning numerous genres, can be successfully navigated using just these core patterns.

The concepts and patterns discussed in this book will form an extensive creative framework for crafting your musical ideas. The goal is to narrow our focus to the vital elements that provide the most creative options. Not only will this give you the biggest return for your effort, but it will also provide the necessary foundations should you later experiment with broader concepts.

In this book, we'll take an in-depth look at fundamental patterns such as octave shapes, the major scale and all its modes, pentatonic scales, blues scales, and various arpeggios (including major seventh, minor seventh, dominant seventh, and more). In addition to outlining and explaining each of these patterns, we'll explore their numerous positions and alternate shapes across the fretboard. We'll also discuss foundational ideas for understanding scales, common uses for each pattern covered, key exercises and techniques for effective learning, and central concepts for using these scales and arpeggios in context.

Each pattern covered in this guide is *movable*, so rather than redundantly outlining every shape in various keys, all scales and arpeggios will be demonstrated from the same starting position, or *root* note, across the fretboard. This has the added benefit of displaying how these patterns are similar and distinct from one another in context.

Lastly, since some concepts introduced may initially feel foreign or difficult, it's important to be conscious of playing fatigue. Be sure to practice at comfortable tempos, and don't forget to take regular breaks when playing. We're going to cover a lot of content, so it's important to work through this book at your own pace. While this information has been streamlined to be easily digestible, the learning process will be different for each person.

1

Foundational Concepts

Before looking at any specific patterns, let's discuss some fundamental concepts regarding scales and how they're used.

Why Scales?

Do we need to learn about scales to make music? The short answer is *no*. In a book about guitar scales, this may seem an unexpected answer. The truth is, creating music can be as simple as playing something you like the sound of. This is, after all, how most of us judge music as listeners. The deciding factor isn't usually whether we can make sense of it theoretically, but simply whether we think it sounds good.

Scales will be of little help if we lose sight of the fact that music is ultimately a *creative* endeavor. Having said that, it would be a mistake to conclude that scales are therefore not important. In creating anything musical, we're already engaging with scales, whether or not we know it. Scales are the basis for everything we do on guitar. They're foundational to things like improvisation, songwriting, arranging, understanding theory, and building technique. For guitar players, scales are a vital part of the language of music.

Scales are an essential tool for understanding how things are connected on the guitar neck. Beyond the obvious benefit practicing scales holds for tasks like developing technique and finger dexterity, understanding scales is fundamental for fretboard navigation. Being able to play effortlessly in any position on the fretboard, regardless of the key, is the byproduct of a solid grounding in guitar scales.

Learning scales not only provides a framework to help communicate our musical ideas, but it also opens the door to new creative possibilities. The belief that theory somehow inhibits creativity is a misconception. In most cases, the reverse is likely true: A lack of understanding will stifle creative potential. Many guitarists feel stuck playing the same old patterns and licks simply because *they can't use what they don't know*. Creative freedom comes from engaging and experimenting with the fundamentals, not from ignoring them.

Understanding Scales

For many, the topic of guitar scales can be daunting. While this is a reflection of the sheer number of scales that exist, it's also symptomatic of the way scales are commonly taught. As guitar players, we tend to think of scales simply as *shapes* on the fretboard. Although this is helpful from a practical standpoint, it gives little indication of what they are and how we might apply them.

The best place to start in understanding scales is actually not to start with *scales* at all. While scales are foundational, *intervals* are the real building blocks of music. An interval is the distance from one note to another. Even a slight shift in this relationship can create an entirely different mood or feel. Major and minor chords, for example, are theoretically just one half step away from being the same chord. It's this slight movement in the middle interval (the flattened 3rd) that dramatically changes the chord's character:

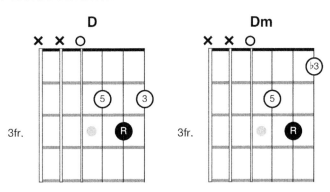

Simply put, a scale is a series of notes with *fixed* intervals. This means the structure these notes follow doesn't change, even when the scale is played in different keys. (This is why most scale shapes on guitar are movable.) It's this fixed sequence of intervals that evokes a scale's unique tonal flavor, or sonic personality, for composing or improvising. Like chords, scales can contain many of the same notes, but it's the slight differences that give a scale its distinct character.

In the Western world, there are only 12 notes in the musical alphabet. The endless creative options available to us come from the way we position these notes in relation to one another. Technically, we use patterns to visualize how notes can be grouped together on the fretboard. Creatively, however, it's more useful to think of a scale as describing a distinct *sound* or *mood*, rather than simply referring to a particular shape.

Tip: *Sometimes it's helpful to think about playing music in the same way we listen to it. When listening to music, we're not concentrating on shapes or positions; we're focused on sounds and emotions. While the technical aspects of learning an instrument are undeniably important, they're less significant than the ability to communicate something through the notes being played.*

Using Scales

As already established, guitar players tend to learn about scales *visually*. However, just being shown what they look like on the guitar fretboard doesn't actually help us use them. While scales are typically taught and practiced in ascending or descending sequences, this isn't how they're used in real-world situations. An audience will rarely care how many scales you know or how fast you can play them! The whole point of learning this information is to create something with it. Scales are simply the palette from which we express our musical ideas.

Guitar players are commonly confused about when and how to use scales. Unfortunately, scales aren't all that helpful if we don't understand how to apply them. In part, this confusion occurs because we're often taught to view chords and scales as separate entities that have different functions. A common example of this is the question: Do you play rhythm or lead guitar? While in a practical sense chords suit rhythm playing and scales suit lead playing, theoretically they're both derived from the same place. As already stated, *intervals* are the fundamental building blocks of music. We use them to create *both* melody and harmony. Chords and scales are therefore intrinsically related.

When we talk about playing in a particular key, we mean that notes used to construct chords and melodies relate to the same fixed sequence of intervals. A practical way to view this relationship would be to say that we build chords *using* scales. For example, all chords in the key of G major are built exclusively from notes within the G major scale and vice versa. This is why melodic ideas structured around the G major scale will work over a G major chord progression. They're both drawing on the same collection of common notes. It's this inherent chord/scale connection that forms the missing link where many players become confused.

To reiterate, scales are used to create both *rhythmic* and *melodic* structures. A songwriter will (knowingly or unknowingly) compose the melodic and harmonic elements of their song based on the mood or personality of a particular scale. As lead guitarists, our contribution to a song often comes after the chord progression has been established. Our task, then, is to find the appropriate scale (or *scales*) to base our melodic ideas on from notes within the chords being played.

Tip: *In many cases, this is relatively straightforward, since numerous progressions in popular music tend to stay within a single key center. However, it's not uncommon for a progression to temporarily borrow chords from another key signature or move to another key entirely. In these situations, our choice of scales needs to be informed by the specific chords being used, not just a single overall key center.*

Learning Scales

Before delving into the patterns covered in this guide, it makes sense first to lay down some ground rules. While there are no *overnight* solutions for learning scales on guitar, there are several learning habits that make this process much easier. In short, the task isn't simply about memorizing endless shapes on the fretboard. We want to understand how these patterns are built, how they function, and how they relate to one another. Below are some key guidelines to consider:

- **One at a Time:** Learning scales isn't a race! Focus on learning and using one shape at a time. It's far more beneficial knowing a handful of patterns really well than knowing many of them poorly. Ensure you can create something musical out of each shape before moving on to the next.

- **Play Slowly:** Playing scales *fast* isn't the initial goal; playing them *accurately* is. Start by practicing slowly at a comfortable tempo and increase speed only when each pattern can be played cleanly. Remember, playing *fast* is different from playing *badly at a fast tempo*.

- **Don't Practice Mistakes:** When we consistently practice something on guitar, we form playing habits. Pay attention to your playing and get used to correcting mistakes, not *practicing* them. Focus on playing things accurately, being mindful of both the tone and tuning of each note.

- **Learn to Self-Correct:** Rather than being frustrated by limitations, learn from them. These challenges teach us to see gaps in our understanding or issues with our technique. The roadblocks we encounter in our playing are signs telling us what to work on next.

- **Focus on Root Notes:** Always remember that we're learning scales, not just *shapes*. The root note forms the tonal center of a scale. As such, it's the central anchor point for our melodic ideas. Understanding the sound and structure of a scale is vital for applying it musically.

- **Look for Shortcuts:** While they can seem like endless amounts of information to memorize, in reality scale patterns include a large amount of repetition. Often, one shape will have multiple applications. Paying attention to these similarities will help streamline the learning process.

- **Make It Musical:** Scales don't always have to be practiced the same way. Make it interesting! Try alternating the rhythm, note sequence, tempo, or dynamics being used. Be sure to play along with songs or make use of jam tracks. Remember, learning scales is never the end goal–making music is.

- **Play in Context:** Don't just practice playing scales; practice hearing and using them *in context*. Listening to and experimenting with the ways other guitarists use these patterns musically is essential for developing your own creative vocabulary on guitar.

- **Repetition Is Key:** Learning scales isn't a difficult task, but it's a *repetitive* one. Consistent practice is key. Be sure to prioritize shorter, more regular practice sessions over longer, more infrequent ones.

- **Be Intentional:** Sometimes, learning something effectively isn't just about the time we spend; it's about *how* we spend our time. Ultimately, focused practice is efficient practice. Be mindful of each specific thing you're looking to improve, and then structure your practice time accordingly.

2

Octave Shapes

Having covered some foundational concepts for learning and using scales, we'll now introduce five key reference points for working with these patterns on the fretboard.

Using Octave Shapes

As already stated, this handbook relates to the various patterns rooted in the diatonic world. Another way of saying this is that each scale and arpeggio covered is connected to the major scale. This is a simple yet extremely important concept to grasp. While scales and arpeggios are often learned or memorized as *unrelated* patterns, this isn't how they function. A pentatonic scale, for example, is basically the major scale minus a few notes. Similarly, both modes and arpeggios are also formed from notes within the major scale.

In short, these shapes are all closely related. While each pattern can be used in isolation, it's important to learn how they overlap and interconnect with one another on the fretboard. Failing to understand this will introduce roadblocks in navigating these patterns effectively when improvising or songwriting. One of the biggest problems in learning to visualize scale shapes as separate patterns is that it's easy to lose sight of how to connect them back up again. Fortunately, there's a simple solution to this problem. It starts with focusing on how each pattern is *similar* before outlining what makes them distinct.

For example, the A minor scale, A minor pentatonic scale, and A minor arpeggio all contain overlapping notes. Here we're primarily interested in the foundational note common to all these shapes, the root note A. While these patterns form distinct shapes on the fretboard, they all revolve around the same starting point. Therefore, even though the overall shape of each pattern will change, the shape created by the root notes within each pattern will not.

Why is this important to understand? Simply put, root notes are foundational to the structure of any scale or arpeggio. In the following section, we'll see that when any note is mapped out across the fretboard, it creates *five* unique octave shapes. These distinct shapes remain consistent, regardless of our starting note. Therefore, it's logical that any scale or arpeggio must be built around one of these five shapes. This will be true no matter what key we're playing in or our position on the fretboard.

As such, all patterns demonstrated in the following chapters of this book will be anchored to one of these octave shapes. This means that each octave shape acts as a basic reference point for visualizing how the numerous patterns covered relate to one another. Understanding this fact enables us to creatively interchange between using modes with pentatonic scales and arpeggios when playing in particular areas on the fretboard.

Tip: *Learning where the root notes are positioned within each scale or arpeggio provides a visual anchor for understanding how these patterns overlap and interconnect. This concept is often discussed in reference to the CAGED system, as these octave shapes also form the basis of our basic C, A, G, E, and D open chords.*

Octave Shapes

Position 1

Position 2

Position 3

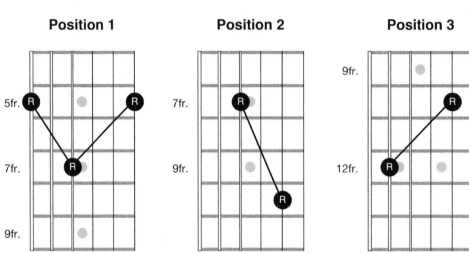

Position 4

Position 5

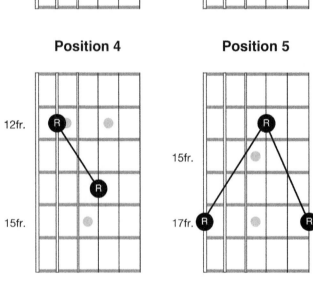

3

Modes

Now that we've covered the groundwork, let's continue by discussing the modes of the major scale.

Understanding Modes

In this chapter, we'll start by looking at the seven modes of the major scale. These patterns form an important foundation for understanding both music theory and fretboard navigation. As such, they'll provide the fundamental framework for exploring all the other diatonic patterns covered in this book. Here's a brief overview describing the structure and sound of each scale.

Note: *Type* refers to the overall tonality of the scale. *Formula* explains the intervallic structure of the scale. *Structure* describes the half-step (one-fret) and whole-step (two-fret) movements within the scale. And *description* briefly outlines the unique tonal character of the scale.

The Ionian Mode (Major Scale)

- **Type:** Major

- **Formula:** R - 2 - 3 - 4 - 5 - 6 - 7

- **Structure:** W - W - H - W - W - W - H

- **Description:** More commonly known as the *major* scale, the Ionian mode is the parent scale to all other modes. Sonically, it has a familiar, triumphant, and cheerful quality.

The Dorian Mode

- **Type:** Minor

- **Formula:** R - 2 - ♭3 - 4 - 5 - 6 - ♭7

- **Structure:** W - H - W - W - W - H - W

- **Description:** Built from the 2nd note (or *degree*) of the major scale, the Dorian mode is essentially a minor scale without the flattened 6th interval. While this mode is categorized as minor, it has a distinctly brighter, bluesier tonality.

The Phrygian Mode

- **Type:** Minor

- **Formula:** R - ♭2 - ♭3 - 4 - 5 - ♭6 - ♭7

- **Structure:** H - W - W - W - H - W - W

- **Description:** Built from the 3rd degree of the major scale, the Phrygian mode is essentially a minor scale with a flattened 2nd. This mode sounds dark and exotic; it's often described as having a uniquely Spanish sound.

The Lydian Mode

- **Type:** Major

- **Formula:** R - 2 - 3 - #4 - 5 - 6 - 7

- **Structure:** W - W - W - H - W - W - H

- **Description:** Built from the 4th degree of the major scale, the Lydian mode is essentially a major scale with a raised 4th. The Lydian mode is often described as having a mysterious and dreamy quality.

The Mixolydian Mode

- **Type:** Major

- **Formula:** R - 2 - 3 - 4 - 5 - 6 - ♭7

- **Structure:** W - W - H - W - W - H - W

- **Description:** Built from the 5th degree of the major scale, the Mixolydian mode is essentially a major scale with a flattened 7th. Sometimes called the *dominant* mode, it sounds similar to the major scale, just with a slightly funkier tonality.

The Aeolian Mode (Minor Scale)

- **Type:** Minor

- **Formula:** R - 2 - ♭3 - 5 - 4 - ♭6 - ♭7

- **Structure:** W - H - W - W - H - W - W

- **Description:** Built from the 6th degree of the major scale, the Aeolian mode is usually referred to as the *minor* or *natural minor* scale. This mode is known for its dramatic or moody sonic quality.

The Locrian Mode

- **Type:** Diminished

- **Formula:** R - ♭2 - ♭3 - 4 - ♭5 - ♭6 - ♭7

- **Structure:** H - W - W - H - W - W - W

- **Description:** Built from the 7th degree of the major scale, the Locrian mode is sometimes called the *half-diminished* mode. It has a dissonant and unstable sound and as such is the least widely used of all the modes.

Using Modes

The modes are commonly misunderstood; they're a popular subject of confusion and debate. Like the pentatonic scales we'll look at, the modes can be broadly categorized under two main types: *major* and *minor* (with the exception of the Locrian mode). Unlike pentatonic scales, however, modal scales are more nuanced and detailed in their tonal character. While this isn't intended to be a detailed theoretical guide, here we'll attempt to ease some of the confusion around this subject.

First, let's clarify the term *modes*. What we're actually referring to are the modes of the *major scale*. This indicates that there's an intrinsic relationship between each modal pattern. Seen from the simplest standpoint, modes are essentially different *inversions* of the same major scale. The mode just refers to our starting point within that scale. For example, the second mode of C major (D Dorian) uses the same notes, but it starts and ends on the 2nd degree of the scale. Put simply, it's the same scale played from a different position.

> **Tip:** *Why is knowing this helpful? Because we can get considerably more mileage from a single scale. Learning to navigate the alternate positions of the major scale allows us to play in any key, from any point along the entire guitar neck!*

In this context, the modes are viewed *relative* to one another. This is usually how they're applied over major and minor chord progressions that stay within one key center. In these situations, practically speaking, there's no real sonic distinction between one mode and another. They each function more as alternate positions of each other, rather than as distinct scales in their own right. For example, playing the third mode of C major (E Phrygian) over a C major progression will still basically sound like the C major scale.

So if each mode uses the same notes, what makes them sound different? Theoretically, because each mode has a different starting point, this shift in the intervals gives each scale a different sound. However, in practice, the distinct character of each mode is apparent only when chords and melodies are structured to emphasize this new *tonal center*. In simple terms, this means the tonality of a scale will change depending on the chords being played. For example, you'll often hear modes being used over a static chord to emphasize their unique sonic quality (e.g., D Dorian over a Dm chord vamp).

Similarly, diatonic progressions can be structured to emphasize the sound of any one of the modes. Here a progression uses the chords of the parent major key but *implies* the sound of a particular mode by revolving around an alternate root (or *tonic*) chord within the scale. Again, the notes being used are the same, but the tonal center being emphasized is different. For example, implying the sound of F major using only the notes and chords from the C major scale would give us an F Lydian sound (F being the 4th degree of C major). This provides a distinctly different sonic quality to a standard F major scale.

Non-diatonic situations are where things get even more interesting. Where a progression moves outside a singular key center, modal scales are commonly used in *parallel* with one another. For example, if a progression were to change key from C to G, the scale used would also need to change to reflect this shift. It may seem obvious just to play the major scales attached to each key center (C major to G major). When playing, however, jumping around to different positions on the fretboard isn't a practical solution. Instead, using the mode of G major that most closely relates to C (the fifth mode, C Mixolydian) provides a much smoother transition. C major and C Mixolydian are similar scales; they start from the same root note, share many common tones, and occupy the same space on the fretboard. This means they can seamlessly interchange with one another.

Finally, a more advanced use of this parallel concept can include *superimposing* one mode where another would be more expected. This involves temporarily substituting one parallel mode for another, not to navigate a key change but to add further tension and interest where desired. Using an E Dorian scale for a *bluesier* sound over an E7 chord (which usually implies the sound of E Mixolydian) would be an example of this. Keep in mind that while this concept certainly adds a different flavor to your melodic ideas, if done carelessly the results can be unpleasant.

Summary

To recap, despite not being a comprehensive overview of the modes, this has hopefully clarified some of the ways they're often used. We can summarize these common applications for modes as follows:

- **Used Over Diatonic Progressions:** Modal patterns are commonly used to play over any major or minor progression that stays within a single key center.

- **Used Over Single-Chord Vamps:** The modes are often applied over a single-chord vamp, where a static chord is used to emphasize the tonal center of a particular modal scale.

- **Used Over Modal Progressions:** Modal scales are often used over diatonic progressions that center around an alternate tonic chord, implying the sound of one key by using the notes and chords from another key.

- **Used Over Key Changes:** The modes can be used to seamlessly navigate through key changes within a song, without jumping around to alternate positions on the fretboard.

- **Used in Parallel:** Substituting one parallel mode (a different mode starting from the same root note) over another is a device used to add further interest or color to a melodic pattern where desired.

Tip: *Notice that despite the various diagrams following this section, each mode repeats the same seven patterns on the fretboard. The only thing that changes is the tonal center of each pattern. For example, over an A minor progression, the C major scale will sound like A minor. Logically, if our melodic ideas gravitate to the sound of A minor, it makes sense that A is the root note, not C.*

Playing Modes

Modal scales can be played in various ways across the fretboard. Here we'll favor an approach that uses three notes per string. Not only do these shapes give us greater reach within a single position, but they also accommodate increased speed and fluidity in our playing. Below we can use the A major scale to demonstrate what this approach looks like when ascending and descending through the root position.

Example 3.1

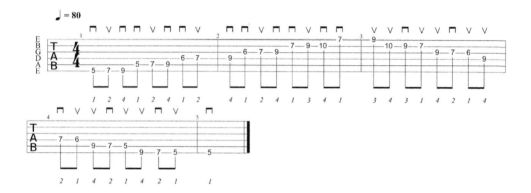

Finger Position

This pattern highlights the three basic movements our left hand will encounter when playing three notes per string. These are:

- Three notes separated by a whole step each (W - W).

- Three notes separated by a half step and then a whole step (H - W).

- Three notes separated by a whole step and then a half step (W - H).

In these situations, the suggested fingerings are:

- Using the 1st, 2nd, and 4th fingers for both W - W and H - W movements.

- Using the 1st, 3rd, and 4th fingers for W - H movements.

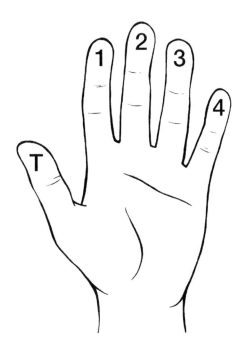

Note: Three-note-per-string shapes might feel foreign at first. Initially, it may be helpful to practice playing these scales higher on the neck, where the fret spacing is closer.

Picking Technique

While standard downstrokes/upstrokes (or *alternate* picking) could be used with these patterns, the previous example demonstrates a different approach. *Economy* picking is a popular technique applied to sequences using three notes per string. It allows us to play consecutive downstrokes when ascending from one string to another and consecutive upstrokes when descending the alternate way. This enables us to omit unnecessary movements from our picking technique, maximizing both accuracy and speed.

The Ionian Mode

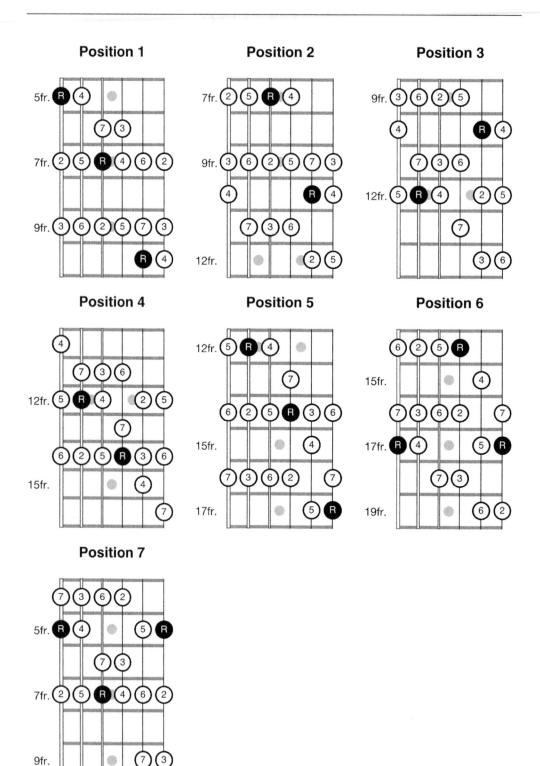

The Dorian Mode

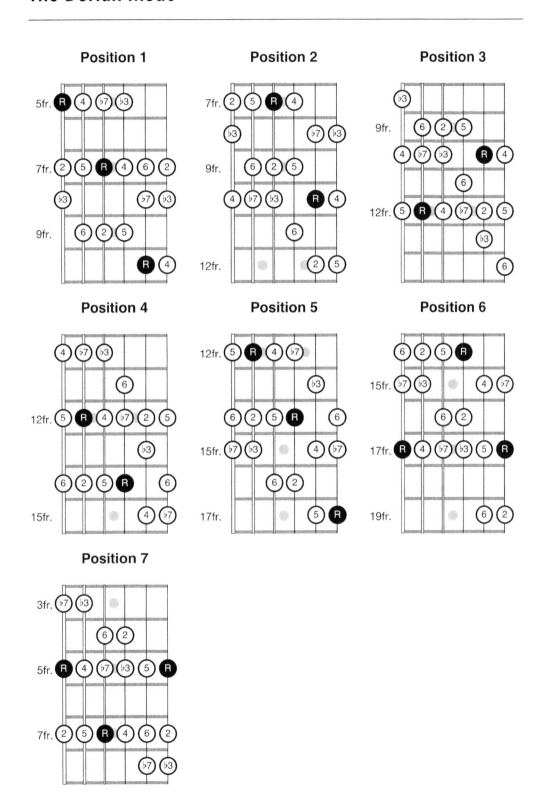

The Phrygian Mode

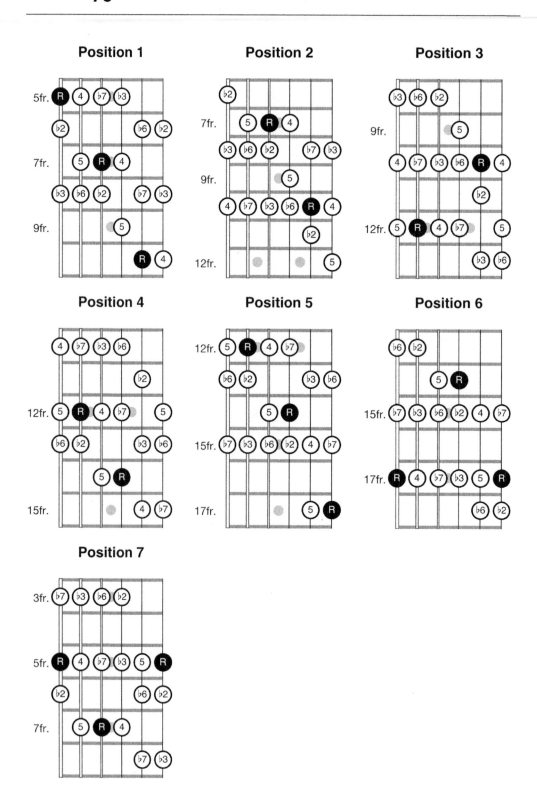

Position 1

Position 2

Position 3

Position 4

Position 5

Position 6

Position 7

The Lydian Mode

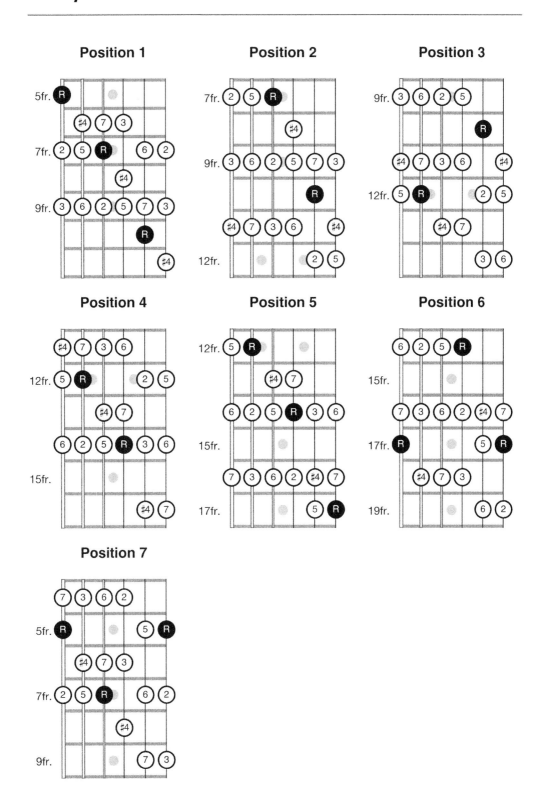

The Mixolydian Mode

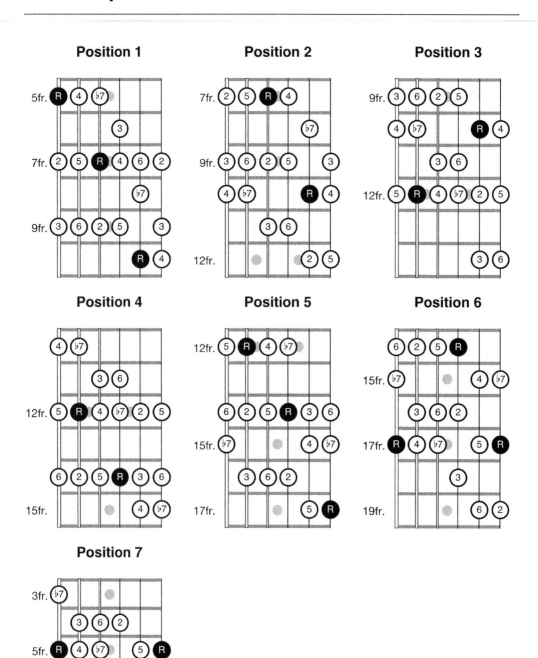

The Aeolian Mode

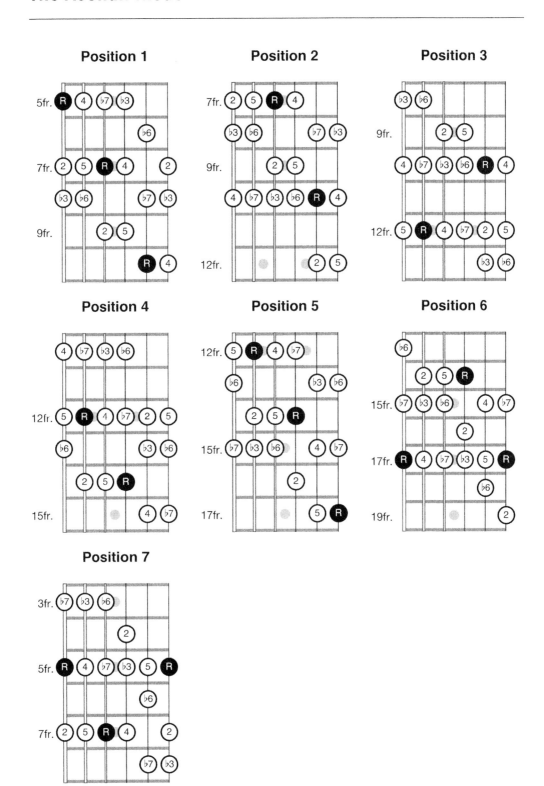

Position 1

Position 2

Position 3

Position 4

Position 5

Position 6

Position 7

The Locrian Mode

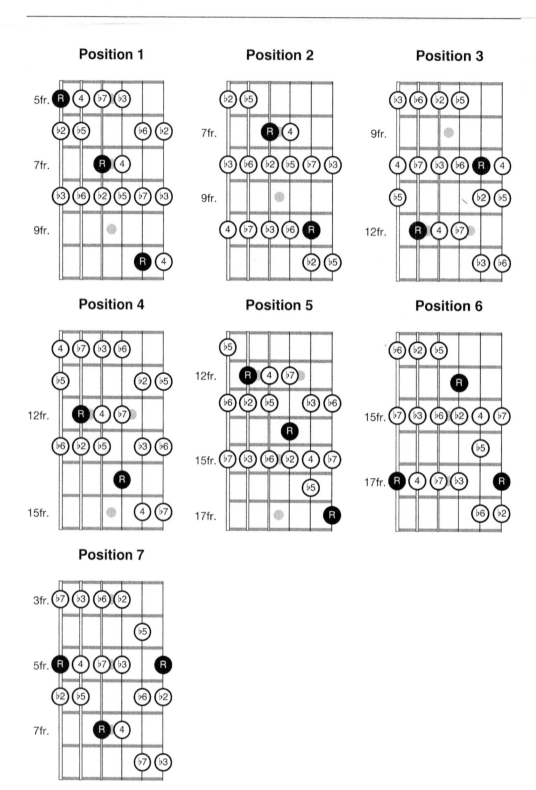

Exercise 1

Start at the 1st position of the major or minor scale and loop through its *relative* positions on the fretboard.

Using a metronome, start at the 3rd fret and play up and back through the G major scale (Ionian) at a comfortable tempo. Repeat this with each subsequent position of G major until you reach the root position again (one octave higher at the 15th fret). After playing once through all seven positions, reverse this exercise to loop through each pattern until you arrive back at the 1st position on the 3rd fret.

Now, repeat this same exercise in the key of G minor. Again, start from the 3rd fret, but this time cycle through each position of the G minor scale (Aeolian).

*Tip: It's highly recommended that you finish each position by playing through the root notes in that pattern. This is very helpful for reinforcing a position's connection with its relative octave shape (covered in **Chapter 2**).*

Exercise 2

Start at the 1st position of the major or minor scale and loop through its *parallel* positions on the fretboard.

Using a metronome, start at the 5th fret and play up and back through the A major scale. Continue by playing through each subsequent mode in *parallel* (e.g., A Dorian, A Phrygian, A Lydian, etc.). Once you have played all seven shapes in parallel, reverse this exercise and loop back through each pattern until you arrive back at the A major scale.

Extra Credit

- Experiment with playing **Exercise 1** using not only the major and minor scales but all the other modes as well. Starting at the 3rd fret, loop through each position of every mode (e.g., G Dorian, G Phrygian, G Lydian, etc.).   ·

- Play **Exercise 1** and **Exercise 2** but avoid ascending and descending through the same position. In other words, try ascending through one pattern and then descending through the next pattern continually in an alternate sequence.

Note: The exercises in this book focus on fretboard navigation. They're designed to work with multiple patterns and positions together. It may take time concentrating on each pattern separately before you can incorporate these larger exercises into your practice.

4

Pentatonic Scales

Having established a broad framework for navigating the fretboard using modes, it's time to explore how this relates to pentatonic scales.

Understanding Pentatonic Scales

In this chapter, we'll discuss the use of pentatonic scales. While, technically, blues scales wouldn't be considered *pentatonic* scales (*penta* implying five notes), they're so commonly used interchangeably with pentatonic scales that it makes sense to include them here. Below is a brief description of each pattern we'll cover:

The Major Pentatonic Scale

- **Type:** Major

- **Formula:** R - 2 - 3 - 5 - 6

- **Structure:** W - W - W+H - W

- **Description:** The major pentatonic scale is essentially a major scale minus the 4th and 7th degrees. It maintains an overall *major* tonality, but the absence of these half-step movements gives this scale a more open sound.

The Major Blues Scale

- **Type:** Major

- **Formula:** R - 2 - ♭3 - 3 - 5 - 6

- **Structure:** W - H - H - W+H - W

- **Description:** Arguably not as popular as the minor blues scale, the major blues scale uses the same notes as a major pentatonic scale, with the addition of a flattened 3rd. Usually used as a passing note, this chromatic tone gives the scale additional color and tension.

The Minor Pentatonic Scale

- **Type:** Minor

- **Formula:** R - ♭3 - 4 - 5 - ♭7

- **Structure:** W+H - W - W - W+H

- **Description:** The minor pentatonic scale is essentially a minor scale minus the 2nd and 6th degrees. As with the major pentatonic, omitting these half-step movements gives the minor pentatonic scale a broader sound.

The Minor Blues Scale

- **Type:** Minor

- **Formula:** R - ♭3 - 4 - ♭5 - 5 - ♭7

- **Structure:** W+H - W - H - H - W+H

- **Description:** Often referred to simply as the *blues scale*, the minor blues scale uses the notes of its minor pentatonic counterpart but adds a flattened 5th. Like the major blues scale, this passing note gives the scale a significantly bluesier character.

Note: Unlike all the other scales and arpeggios covered in this book, blues scales contain non-diatonic notes. In other words, these are *chromatic* notes not found within either parent major or minor scales.

Using Pentatonic Scales

Pentatonic scales are used extensively throughout numerous genres. They're often the first stop for most aspiring lead guitarists. Not only are they easier to play and understand than modal scales, but the lack of any half-step intervals also makes them better suited to wider applications. While this means they're extremely useful, pentatonic scales lack the tonal nuances we find within the modes.

Pentatonic scales are commonly used in place of (or in conjunction with) their parent major or minor scales when improvising or composing. As already mentioned, they're also often used interchangeably with blues scales. While the name may suggest an exclusive association with blues music, this scale is used widely throughout various other genres such as rock and jazz. In practice, this interchange isn't usually viewed as substituting one scale type for another. Rather, it's seen as incorporating colorful *passing notes* from the blues scales to embellish our pentatonic licks and ideas.

Not only are pentatonic scales commonly used to play over an entire progression, but they can also be applied independently over different chords. This involves structuring melodic phrases around multiple pentatonic scales to align with each major or minor chord change in a progression. Using a single pentatonic scale will emphasize the overall tonal center of a progression, whereas using multiple scales will better outline the sound of each specific chord.

Note: Like the octave shapes covered in **Chapter 2**, this technique of connecting pentatonic patterns with individual chord shapes is often referred to as part of the CAGED system.

Additionally, pentatonic scales can be used with other modal scales outside the parent major or minor scales. For example, the major pentatonic scale can be used interchangeably with any of the major modes: Ionian, Lydian, and Mixolydian. Likewise, the minor pentatonic scale can be substituted with any of the minor modes: Dorian, Phrygian, and Aeolian. This is possible because the intervals that differentiate these modes from one another are helpfully omitted in the major and minor pentatonic scales. In other words, pentatonic scales share the same intervals common to each mode, in both major and minor contexts.

Theoretically, for the more advanced player, this concept opens the door to some interesting *substitutions*. When playing over a particular key center, we could technically use pentatonic scales based on any mode within that key. For example, this means that over a C major progression, we could play a *C major* pentatonic scale from the tonic (based on Ionian), an *F major* pentatonic scale from the 4th degree (based on Lydian), or a *G major* pentatonic scale from the 5th degree (based on Mixolydian). All without moving outside notes in the parent major scale! The same concept would also apply when playing in a minor key. However, it's worth noting that while they add some interesting color, substituted pentatonic scales usually sound less *resolved* than those based on the tonic chord of a progression.

This concept of pentatonic substitution can be extended even further. *Parallel* pentatonic scales are commonly used to intentionally move outside what might typically be considered the *safe* notes to play over a chord progression. Examples of this include using minor pentatonic scales over major chords or temporarily substituting parallel major and minor pentatonic scales in place of one another. Both examples are extremely common in blues music.

Summary

While this wasn't intended to be a thorough analysis of pentatonic theory, it has hopefully provided insight into the usefulness and versatility the humble pentatonic scale provides. To summarize, we can recap their popular applications as follows:

- **Used Over Diatonic Progressions:** Pentatonic scales are commonly used in place of their parent major and minor scales when playing over an entire chord progression.

- **Used Over Chord Changes:** Pentatonic scales are often used to emphasize the chord changes in a progression by matching the corresponding pentatonic pattern to each major or minor chord shape.

- **Used Instead of Modes:** Pentatonic scales can be used in place of any major or minor mode, because they're built using the common tones between these scales.

- **Used in Substitution:** Using the modal positions as a reference, various pentatonic scales can be substituted over a single key center, without moving outside the key.

- **Used in Parallel:** Often used for its *bluesy* tonality, parallel major and minor pentatonic scales are commonly played interchangeably for added flavor to melodic ideas.

Tip: Like the modes, both major and minor pentatonic scales use the same patterns on the fretboard; they just start from different positions. In either context, the tonal center or root note is the only thing that changes, not the actual shape.

Playing Pentatonic Scales

It's possible to play pentatonic scales in various ways on the fretboard. By far the most popular method, however, uses five basic *box* shapes. The larger interval gaps in pentatonic scales make them well suited to playing two notes per string (with the exception of additional notes in the blues patterns). While these shapes are arguably less conducive to speed picking, they're easier to play than modal patterns. Below, we can use the A major pentatonic scale to demonstrate what this approach looks like when ascending and descending through the root position.

Example 4.1

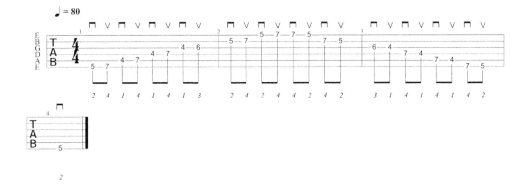

Finger Position

This pattern highlights the two basic movements our left hand will encounter when playing two notes per string in this way. These are:

- Two notes separated by a whole step (W).

- Two notes separated by a whole step plus a half step (W + H).

In these situations, common fingerings include:

- Using the 1st and 3rd fingers for W movements.

- Using the 1st and 4th fingers for W + H movements.

Note: Since pentatonic scales are each contained within a four-fret area on the fretboard, you could alternatively allocate each finger to cover one fret (as demonstrated in the example). In reality, though, once you're familiar with each basic pattern, fingerings often change intuitively depending on what's being played. This is especially true when using additional notes from the blues scales, as these tend to move out of the four-fret box shape.

Picking Technique

Here, alternate picking has been suggested. However, the economy picking technique outlined in **Chapter 3** can be used on select strings when adding notes from the blues scales.

Major Pentatonic Scales

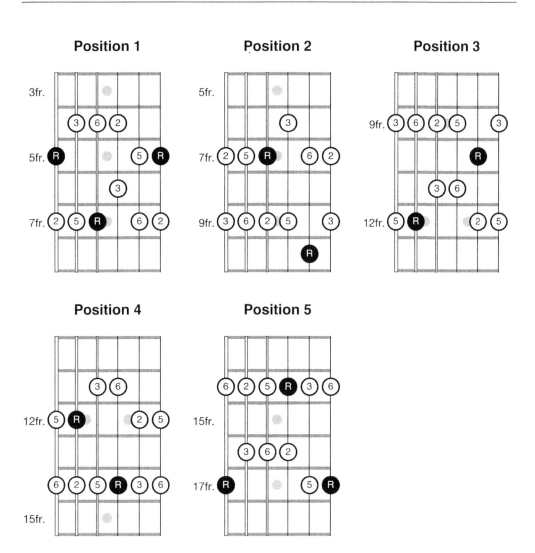

Major Blues Scales

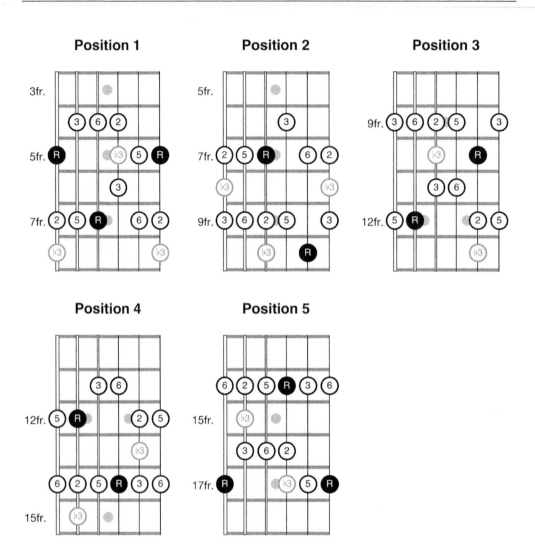

Minor Pentatonic Scales

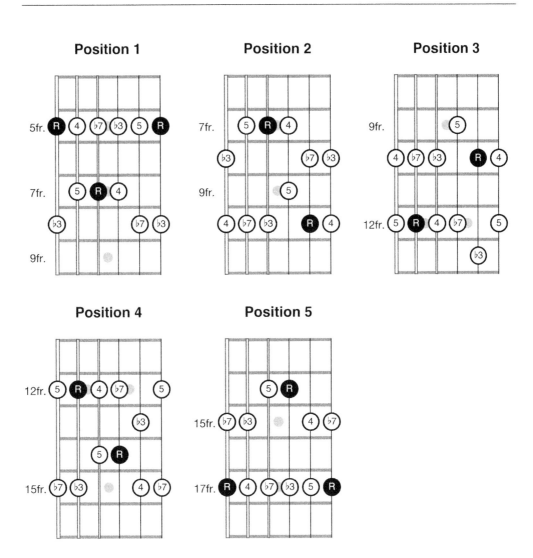

Minor Blues Scales

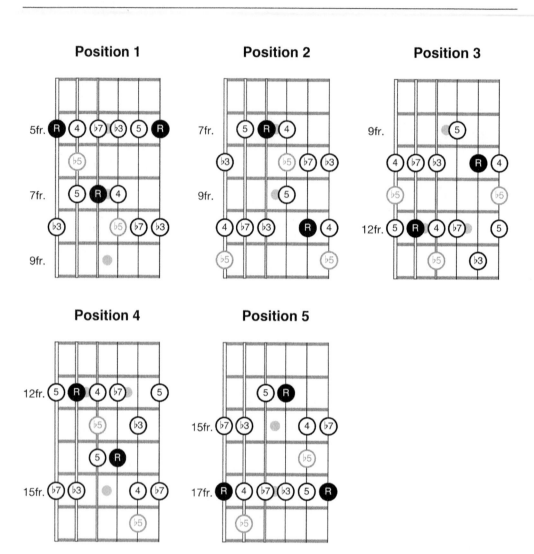

Position 1

Position 2

Position 3

Position 4

Position 5

Exercise 3

Start at the 1ˢᵗ position of the major or minor pentatonic scale and loop through its *relative* positions on the fretboard.

Using a metronome, start at the 3ʳᵈ fret and play up and back through the G major pentatonic scale at a comfortable tempo. Repeat this with each subsequent pentatonic position until you reach the root position again (one octave higher at the 15ᵗʰ fret). After playing once through all five positions, reverse this exercise to loop through each pattern until you arrive back at the 1ˢᵗ position on the 3ʳᵈ fret.

Now, repeat this same exercise in the key of G minor. Again, start from the 3ʳᵈ fret, but this time cycle through each position of the G minor pentatonic scale.

Tip: As with the modal exercises, try finishing each position by playing through the root notes in that pattern. Take careful note of how the modal patterns overlap each pentatonic scale by using the same octave shapes.

Exercise 4

Start at the 1ˢᵗ position of the major or minor pentatonic scale and loop through its *parallel* positions on the fretboard.

Using a metronome, start at the 5ᵗʰ fret and play up and back through the A major pentatonic scale. Continue by playing through each subsequent pentatonic shape in *parallel* (starting from the same fret). Once you have played all five shapes in parallel, reverse this exercise and loop back through each pattern until you arrive back at the A major pentatonic scale.

Extra Credit

- Experiment with playing **Exercise 3** using various keys. If you run out of room on the fretboard, just loop back to the equivalent position one octave lower (below your starting point).

- Repeat both **Exercise 3** and **Exercise 4**. This time try including additional notes from the major and minor blues scales.

5

Arpeggios

After looking at both modes and pentatonic scales, here we'll consider how arpeggios can be used to complement these core patterns.

Understanding Arpeggios

While arpeggios aren't traditionally categorized as *scales*, they're so regularly used in connection with scales (or even in place of them) that it makes sense to give them equal importance. Here's a brief overview of the arpeggios covered in this section:

Major Arpeggio

- **Type:** Major

- **Formula:** R - 3 - 5

- **Structure:** W+W - W+H

- **Description:** The major arpeggio is structured using notes from the basic major chord. It shares intervals common to all major modes and major pentatonic scales.

Minor Arpeggio

- **Type:** Minor

- **Formula:** R - ♭3 - 5

- **Structure:** W+H - W+W

- **Description:** The minor arpeggio is structured using notes from the basic minor chord. It shares intervals common to all minor modes and minor pentatonic scales.

Major Seventh Arpeggio

- **Type:** Major

- **Formula:** R - 3 - 5 - 7

- **Structure:** W+W - W+H - W+W

- **Description:** The major seventh arpeggio embellishes the sound of a major arpeggio, giving it a sweeter, more colorful tonality. It shares intervals common to both the Ionian and Lydian modes.

Minor Seventh Arpeggio

- **Type:** Minor

- **Formula:** R - ♭3 - 5 - ♭7

- **Structure:** W+H - W+W - W+H

- **Description:** The minor seventh arpeggio extends the sound of a minor arpeggio, giving it a richer sonic quality. It's essentially a minor pentatonic scale minus the 4th degree, and it shares intervals common to all minor modes.

Dominant Seventh Arpeggio

- **Type:** Major

- **Formula:** R - 3 - 5 - ♭7

- **Structure:** W+W - W+H - W+H

- **Description:** The dominant seventh arpeggio embellishes the sound of a major arpeggio, this time with a flattened 7th. Sounding less resolved and bluesier than a major seventh arpeggio, it shares intervals common to the Mixolydian mode.

Minor Seven Flat Five Arpeggio

- **Type:** Diminished

- **Formula:** R - ♭3 - ♭5 - ♭7

- **Structure:** W+H - W+H - W+W

- **Description:** Also known as the *half-diminished* arpeggio, this pattern is essentially a minor seventh arpeggio with a flattened 5th. It sounds extremely tense and dissonant and shares intervals common to the Locrian mode.

Using Arpeggios

Heavy use of arpeggios is often synonymous with styles such as classical or jazz. In reality, however, their usefulness far exceeds any one particular genre. In fact, in numerous situations you may find a strong understanding of arpeggios is equally, if not more important than a comprehensive knowledge of scales.

Like scales, arpeggios are a series of notes with fixed intervals. However, unlike scales, arpeggios are composed solely of chord tones. In using arpeggios, we're essentially interpreting chords as scales. Generally, the larger interval gaps we find in chords impart a greater sense of melodic flow into our phrasing. Beyond this, there are several other benefits to this approach.

First, arpeggios can function as a central melodic framework around which we structure our musical ideas. The notes in any scale have a different tonal character in relation to one another. Some sound tense and unresolved, while others sound strong and stable. Although this contrast is an important dynamic in music, *chord tones* are often the more desirable notes to emphasize in a melodic phrase. Centering around and embellishing arpeggio shapes relating to the tonic chord of a key is an extremely useful device for doing this.

Tip: This doesn't mean melodic ideas should only use chord tones. Additional notes are vital for adding color and interest to a melodic passage. It simply implies that chord tones are typically the stronger, more resolved-sounding notes.

Many guitarists also use arpeggios to accent chord tones, not of an overall key, but of each individual chord in a progression. This technique is commonly referred to as *playing over the changes* or *chord-tone soloing*. Similar to the way pentatonic scales are sometimes used, a guitar player will structure their melodic ideas around the arpeggio shapes corresponding to each chord being played. This approach is used to reinforce the mood and momentum of a chord progression. The technique is extremely common in jazz but can also be found throughout numerous other genres.

Additionally, arpeggios can be used to navigate tricky or unexpected chord changes in a progression. For example, if a non-diatonic chord is introduced into a progression, rather than shifting temporarily to a different scale, it's often simpler to use an arpeggio pattern instead. In this way, playing notes from the corresponding arpeggio is useful for navigating potentially awkward changes with minimal fuss and without resorting to alternate scales.

Note: Like chords, arpeggios can be extended or altered. It's common to add chord *extensions* (e.g., 9, 11, or 13) or *alterations* (e.g., ♭5 or ♯5) to arpeggios for added color. This can be used to more accurately mirror the exact chord we're playing over.

Arpeggios can also be used to emphasize *sweet notes* and other interesting tonalities over either a particular chord or an entire progression. In this situation, we can imply the sound of one arpeggio where you might expect to hear another. For example, in the key of E minor, a Gmaj7 arpeggio can be built from the 3rd of an Em7 chord (using notes from the same scale). Rather than clashing, the two will sound harmonious together. This is because a Gmaj7 arpeggio uses notes from the Em7 chord and simply adds the 9th extension on top. While the concept of *superimposing* arpeggios sounds relatively advanced, a little experimentation with this idea can produce some very pleasing results.

Finally, arpeggios can sometimes be used in *parallel.* As with both pentatonic scales and modes, there are situations where you could use seemingly unrelated arpeggios from the same root note. Playing a minor seventh arpeggio over a major blues progression or using a minor seven flat five arpeggio in a minor blues solo are both examples of this. Again, careless use of this type of technique can produce haphazard results.

Summary

As with the other scales covered, the intention hasn't been to provide an exhaustive theoretical analysis. The goal has been to offer some context and explanation of how important these patterns can be for your creative vocabulary on guitar. We can summarize the popular uses for arpeggios as follows:

- **Used as Melodic Devices:** Arpeggios are often used in improvisation and composition for their flowing, chord-based melodic quality.

- **Used Over Chord Changes:** Along with additional melodic embellishments, arpeggios are commonly used to emphasize the chord changes in a progression.

- **Used Over Non-Diatonic Chords:** Arpeggios can be used as a simple way to navigate potentially awkward chord changes without resorting to additional scales.

- **Used in Substitution:** Different arpeggios sharing similar chord tones can be superimposed over a chord or progression to imply a richer harmonic character.

- **Used in Parallel:** Sometimes, seemingly unrelated arpeggios can be used in parallel to add tension or dissonance to a melodic sequence.

Tip: Unlike modes and pentatonic scales, the various arpeggio patterns in the following sections don't reuse the same core shapes. However, like modes and pentatonic scales, they're all based on one of the five octave shapes covered in **Chapter 2***. This means each shape will still share some core similarities.*

Playing Arpeggios

Since arpeggios commonly comprise just three or four notes, there are numerous possibilities for playing them on the fretboard. While arpeggio patterns can be extended across all six strings, they're often broken down and used in numerous smaller variations. Despite this, all arpeggio shapes can be traced to one of five basic chord forms: C, A, G, E, and D. Like scales, each of these patterns also aligns with the fundamental octave shapes covered in **Chapter 2**. Below are two examples that demonstrate this using both the Amaj7 and Am7 arpeggio patterns based around an E barre chord shape.

Example 5.1

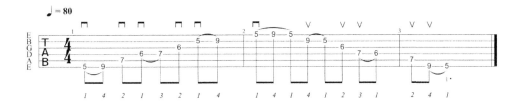

Example 5.2

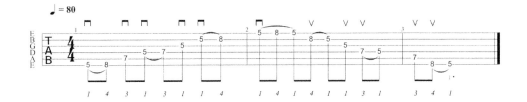

Finger Position

Unlike the scales we've looked at, the following arpeggio patterns will vary broadly when it comes to finger position. Depending on how they're played, arpeggios will often use one, two, and sometimes three notes per string. This will require some creative license as you work through each pattern. However, the previous examples highlight a couple things to keep in mind:

- First, sometimes the position each finger gravitates to naturally may not be the optimal choice for achieving smooth, flowing movements. In the first example, the half-step movement between notes on the 4th string uses the 1st and 3rd fingers. While the 1st and 2nd fingers might feel more natural, this would make it much harder to navigate the rest of the pattern. Try to think a note ahead of the one you're playing.

- Second, arpeggio patterns often use consecutive notes on adjacent frets. As seen between the 2nd and 3rd strings in the second example, this means multiple notes can be fretted by the same finger. This technique is similar to a small barre, except it requires a slight rolling motion so each note sounds cleanly without ringing into another.

Note: Each pattern outlined in the following sections is a highly useful recommendation. However, since there are many ways to play any arpeggio, experimentation with alternate patterns is also encouraged.

Picking Technique

Alternate picking could be applied to these patterns, but this isn't the suggested approach. Instead, *sweep* picking is a popular method that's often used when playing arpeggios. It's an extremely beneficial technique for cultivating fast, smooth movements. As seen in both examples, it requires that all ascending note sequences be downstrokes, and all descending note sequences be upstrokes. This differs from strumming, because all notes are still picked independently and aren't intended to ring into one another. For this to work, not every note can be picked. As shown, it will be necessary in places to make use of *hammer-ons* when ascending and *pull-offs* when descending.

Major Arpeggios

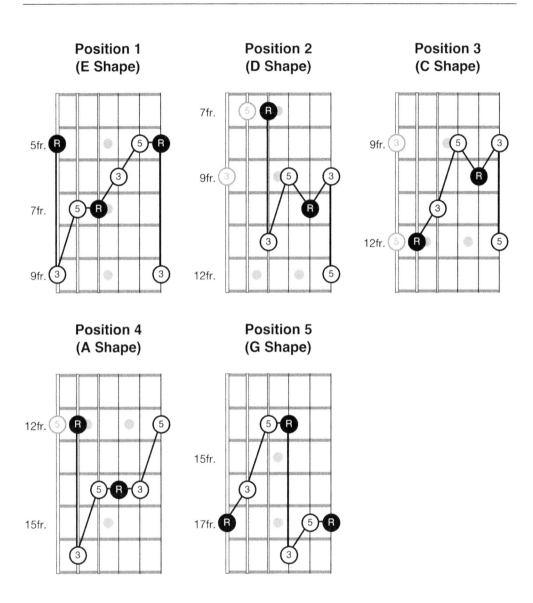

Position 1 (E Shape)
Position 2 (D Shape)
Position 3 (C Shape)
Position 4 (A Shape)
Position 5 (G Shape)

Note: Each pattern is referenced by its relative position to the other scales we've looked at and also by the basic chord type it represents. Since not all chords extend across all strings, the light gray notes show how each pattern can extend below the root note when needed.

Minor Arpeggios

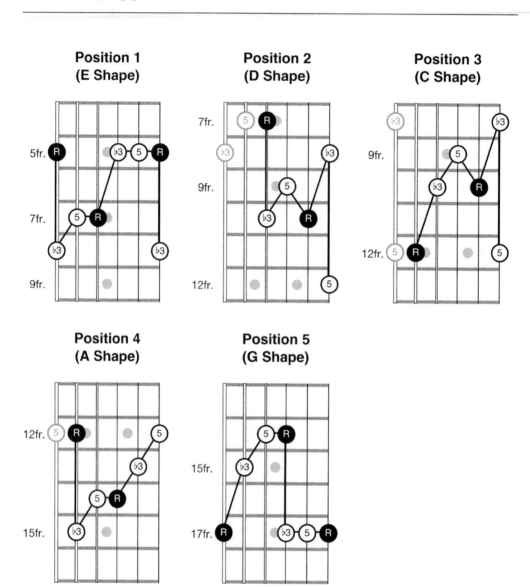

Major Seventh Arpeggios

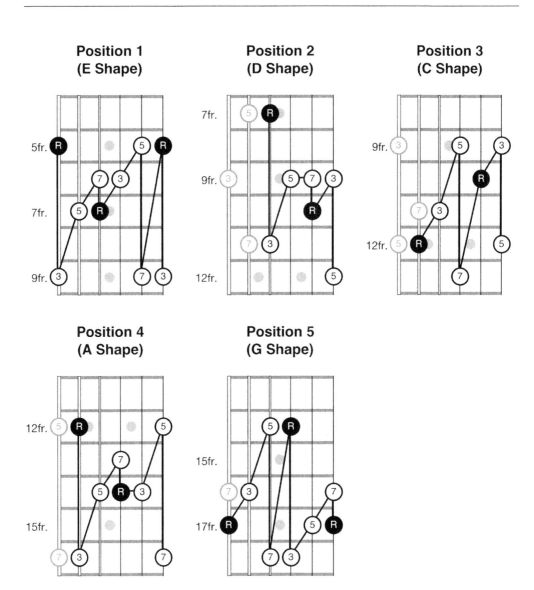

Minor Seventh Arpeggios

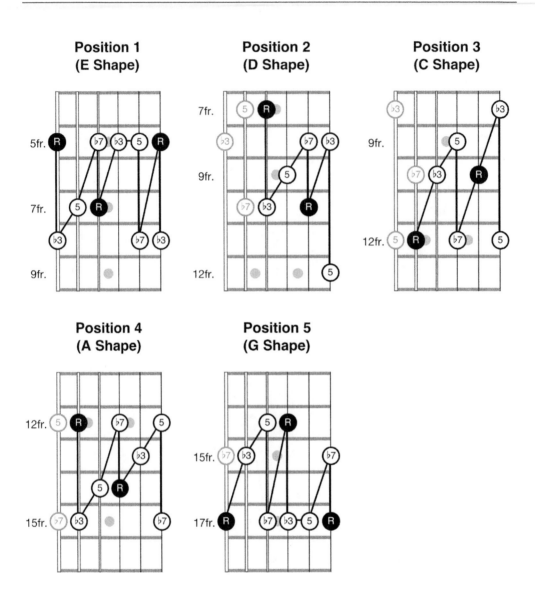

Position 1
(E Shape)

Position 2
(D Shape)

Position 3
(C Shape)

Position 4
(A Shape)

Position 5
(G Shape)

Dominant Seventh Arpeggios

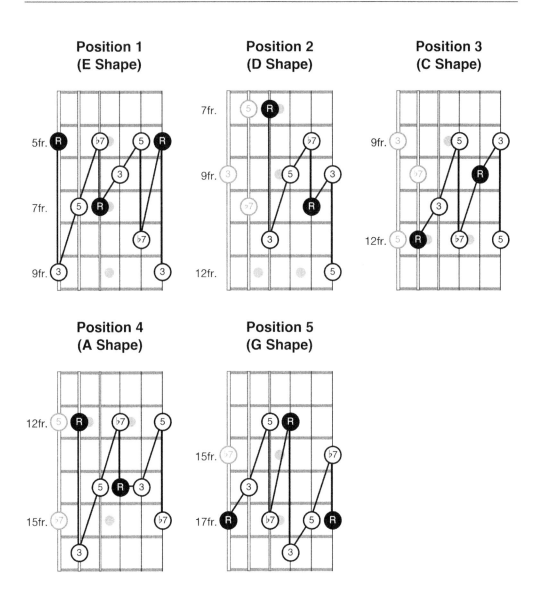

Minor Seven Flat Five Arpeggios

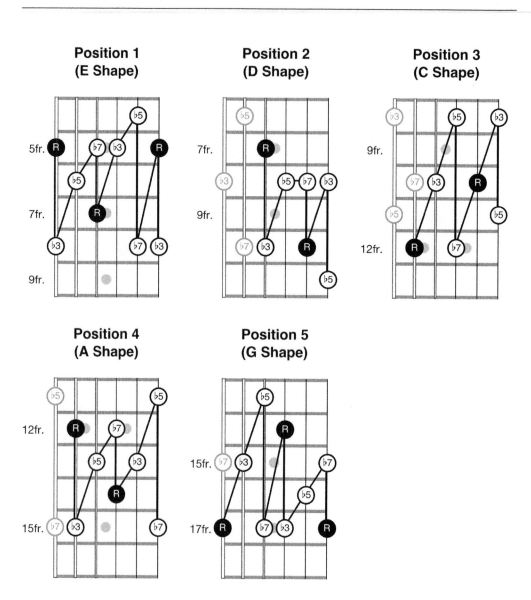

Exercise 5

Start at the E shape of the major or minor arpeggio and loop through its *relative* positions on the fretboard.

Using a metronome, start at the 3rd fret and play up and back through the G major arpeggio (E shape) at a comfortable tempo. Repeat this with each subsequent G major arpeggio (D, C, A, and G shapes) until you reach the E shape again (one octave higher at the 15th fret). After playing once through all five positions, reverse this exercise to loop through each pattern until you arrive back at the E shape on the 3rd fret.

Now, repeat this same exercise in the key of G minor. Again, start from the 3rd fret, but this time cycle through the various G minor arpeggio shapes in sequence.

Tip: As with the other scales, pay attention to the octave shapes within each pattern. This time, however, note the specific chord type (C, A, G, E, or D) that coincides with each unique octave shape. This will be the same for both major and minor arpeggios.

Exercise 6

Start at each position of the major seventh arpeggio and loop through the *parallel* seventh arpeggio patterns on the fretboard.

Using a metronome, start at the 5th fret and play up and back through the Amaj7 arpeggio (E shape). Continue by playing through each *parallel* variation of this seventh arpeggio, starting from the same root note (Am7, A7, and Am7♭5). Once all four shapes have been played in parallel, reverse this exercise and loop back through each pattern until you arrive back at the Amaj7 arpeggio.

Now, repeat this same exercise in each subsequent position of the Amaj7 arpeggio (using each D, C, A, and G shape variation). Again, start from the same root note and this time loop through each seventh arpeggio pattern in parallel.

Extra Credit

- Practice playing **Exercise 5** using not only major and minor arpeggios but all the seventh arpeggio variations as well.

- Experiment with playing **Exercise 6** starting from root notes on the fretboard other than A. Be sure to practice positions both above and below the 12th fret.

6

Scales in Context

Now that many essential concepts for using scales and arpeggios have been covered, let's conclude by looking at these patterns in context.

Thinking in Context

In the previous chapters, we've taken a detailed look at octave shapes, modes, pentatonic scales, and arpeggio patterns. We've also discussed essential concepts for learning scales, looked at popular uses for each pattern, and introduced some key practice exercises.

Admittedly, a significant amount of information has been covered. Since the intention has largely been to stay within the diatonic realm, however, you could say we've been looking at the same group of notes, just from different perspectives. In other words, there's an inherent connection between each pattern covered. Although it's important to learn each one separately, thinking of them merely as *isolated* shapes is significantly less helpful than viewing them in context with one another.

As stated earlier, the key to using these patterns together isn't to focus on their differences but on their similarities. While this will hopefully be apparent by now, below is a chart summarizing how these patterns are compatible with one another when improvising or songwriting.

Compatibility Guide

Modal Scale	Pentatonic Scale	Arpeggio Pattern
Ionian *R - 2 - 3 - 4 - 5 - 6 - 7*	Major/Major Blues *R - 2 - (b3) - 3 - 5 - 6*	Major/Major 7th *R - 3 - 5 - (7)*
Dorian *R - 2 - b3 - 4 - 5 - 6 - b7*	Minor/Minor Blues *R - b3 - 4 - (b5) - 5 - b7*	Minor/Minor 7th *R - b3 - 5 - (b7)*
Phrygian *R - b2 - b3 - 4 - 5 - b6 - b7*	Minor/Minor Blues *R - b3 - 4 - (b5) - 5 - b7*	Minor/Minor 7th *R - b3 - 5 - (b7)*
Lydian *R - 2 - 3 - #4 - 5 - 6 - 7*	Major/Major Blues *R - 2 - (b3) - 3 - 5 - 6*	Major/Major 7th *R - 3 - 5 - (7)*
Mixolydian *R - 2 - 3 - 4 - 5 - 6 - b7*	Major/Major Blues *R - 2 - (b3) - 3 - 5 - 6*	Major/Dominant 7th *R - 3 - 5 - (b7)*
Aeolian *R - 2 - b3 - 4 - 5 - b6 - b7*	Minor/Minor Blues *R - b3 - 4 - (b5) - 5 - b7*	Minor/Minor 7th *R - b3 - 5 - (b7)*
Locrian *R - b2 - b3 - 4 - b5 - b6 - b7*	Minor Blues (no 5th) *R - b3 - 4 - b5 - b7*	Diminished/Minor 7b5 *R - b3 - b5 - (b7)*

To reiterate, pentatonic scales are made up of notes common to each of their respective major or minor modes. Likewise, both pentatonic scales and modes share intervals common to the basic major and minor arpeggios. Additionally, each minor mode is compatible with all minor seventh arpeggios, with only two of the major modes being compatible with major seventh arpeggios. In contrast, the flattened 7th in the Mixolydian mode gives it a dominant seventh tonality.

Note: The Locrian mode is the odd one out. It isn't compatible with either major or minor pentatonic scales or their respective arpeggios. However, if we omit the natural 5th, the minor blues scale can be interchanged with the Locrian mode.

Playing in Context

In this guide, we've explored visualizing various pattern *types* along with numerous pattern *positions*. In total, this equates to almost 100 different positions on the fretboard, spread across 17 distinct scales and arpeggios. While this can seem intimidating, in reality working with this information is less complicated than it may appear.

As previously emphasized, not only is there a large amount of repetition between patterns, but each pattern can be reduced to one of five octave shapes (outlined in **Chapter 2**). To put this in perspective, below is a chart summarizing how each octave shape relates to the various positions of every pattern covered. Hopefully, now that you've worked through the previous chapters, these connections should be reasonably obvious. However, as a reference it's helpful to summarize how each position overlaps the others in context.

Navigation Guide

Octave Shape	Pentatonic Scale	Modal Scale	Arpeggio Pattern
Shape 1	Position 1	Positions 1 & 7	E Shape
Shape 2	Position 2	Position 2	D Shape
Shape 3	Position 3	Position 3	C Shape
Shape 4	Position 4	Positions 4 & 5	A Shape
Shape 5	Position 5	Position 6	G Shape

Note: While pentatonic scales and arpeggios fit neatly over the five octave shapes, modes will overlap the same reference point in a few positions. Also, each pattern in this chart is only categorized *generally*. This is because these respective positions will align, regardless of the specific pentatonic scale, mode, or arpeggio pattern used. (In all mode variations, the *relative* positions stay the same.)

> *Tip:* The emphasis here is how these patterns can be used interchangeably. This doesn't mean you need to use each pattern in every situation. It simply indicates that being aware of the way they're related on the fretboard provides more creative options for crafting melodic ideas.

Practicing in Context

As you become more familiar with each pattern, it's important to begin practicing them in context with one another. Until this point, each exercise in this book has centered around two key concepts: practicing in *relative* positions and practicing in *parallel* positions. Visualizing the relative positions of any scale pattern is central in fretboard navigation, allowing you to play over any key using any position on the guitar neck. Being able to visualize multiple parallel patterns within a single playing position is essential for playing over chord changes and seamlessly navigating through multiple keys.

While these are fundamental concepts for practicing scales, moving forward it's extremely beneficial to develop your own personalized playing routines. Ideally, you want to practice applying these patterns in real musical situations, not only by themselves, but also with one another. How you do this will depend largely on your preferred starting point for visualizing the fretboard.

If you're used to playing pentatonic scales, look at how the modal positions and arpeggio patterns overlap these core shapes you're already familiar with. If you favor the three-note-per-string framework, try incorporating different pentatonic and arpeggio licks into each modal position. If you like the chord-centered approach, focus on arpeggio patterns and practice embellishing them with notes from the surrounding pentatonic and modal scales.

Essentially, these are just different ways of working with the same information, but it's helpful to know which starting point seems the most logical to you. In general, a comprehensive practice routine might involve working through the mode, pentatonic scale, and arpeggio connected to each octave shape in all five positions on the fretboard. While the specifics of each pattern will change depending on the mode, the relative positions will stay the same.

Tip: Each mode will interact with pentatonic scales and arpeggios in a slightly different way. Initially, it may be helpful to focus on interchanging patterns using major and minor scales before working with the other modes.

Ultimately, there are no *rules* for putting together your own practice routines. Other helpful practice habits might include practicing in different keys at various tempos, limiting yourself to specific areas on the fretboard, navigating through patterns using only two or three strings, or working with patterns linearly across a single string. Any exercise that helps you engage with these patterns from different perspectives is positive. Since musicality is always the goal, practicing in the context of songs and real playing situations will be of the most benefit.

Note: Want more help with this? Be sure to check out **5-Minute Guitar Jams** as a supplementary practice guide. This book features an album of high-quality backing tracks to accompany your practice.

Final Thoughts

Congratulations on completing *Learn Your Guitar Scales*!

If you've worked closely through each section, you'll now have a comprehensive framework for navigating the fretboard, crafting melodic ideas, and enhancing your improvisational skills. The intention hasn't been to overwhelm you with an encyclopedia of scale patterns (many of which you may never actually use). Instead, the goal has been to focus comprehensively on the core elements that are likely to form the bulk of your musical vocabulary on guitar.

This isn't to say a broader knowledge of scales won't be useful in certain situations, but simply that the greatest impact on your playing usually comes from understanding these central scale and arpeggio patterns. Beyond merely giving you shapes to memorize, the purpose has been to look at these patterns in context, discuss their common uses, and offer various tips and exercises for working practically with this information.

I sincerely hope this guide has helped answer questions, introduce new ideas, and lay solid foundations for ongoing study and experimentation. While a lot of ground has been covered, always remember: What we know is substantially less important than what we *do* with what we know. Learning scales isn't the same as making music, just as learning words isn't the same as talking. Both can open an entire world of creative potential, but neither makes sense unless they're being used to communicate or express something.

May this book help inspire you toward continued learning and creativity.

5-MINUTE GUITAR JAMS

Backing Tracks

JAM TRACKS FOR ROCK & BLUES GUITAR

LUKE ZECCHIN

This book is dedicated to all the friends and musicians I've had the privilege of playing with. Thank you for making me better.

Published by **GuitarIQ.com**

Copyedited by Jason Whited

Proofread by Dan Foster

Illustrated by Jasmin Zecchin

Contents

Preface

Welcome, and thank you for choosing *5-Minute Guitar Jams*.

Often, the way we practice is disconnected from how we actually use the guitar in real-world situations. In what circumstance would someone stand alone in front of an audience, set the metronome going, and proceed to play a variety of scales and technique-building exercises? Who'd pay to listen to that? As necessary as these types of exercises are for our development as musicians, they're never the end goal.

Mastering anything requires practice; that much has always been clear. Unfortunately, the notion of *practice* is often viewed negatively, as if it's some inherently difficult or tedious task. This mindset has far more to do with our approach to learning rather than the *learning* itself. Simply put, practicing guitar should be enjoyable because playing guitar should be enjoyable! The two are inseparable. If there's a split between our enjoyment of playing and our motivation to practice, then perhaps we need to rethink our approach to practicing in the first place.

The concept behind *5-Minute Guitar Jams* is simple. The whole point of learning how to play guitar is to do something *musical* with that skill. The collection of backing tracks that accompany this handbook are aimed at creating a more realistic playing environment for practicing improvisation, scale patterns, and other technical exercises.

The goal of this short guide is to help you get the most from using these backing tracks. This includes taking a detailed look at each of the progressions used and outlining numerous scale options for improvisation. Beyond this, the aim is to help refine your playing skills by becoming more intentional with your practice time. In short, this handbook will encourage a fresh way of thinking about practicing that's both engaging and effective.

I sincerely hope this guide assists you in using your practice time more constructively and ignites renewed excitement in your playing.

—Luke Zecchin

Introduction

Jam tracks for guitar players aren't a new concept. The appeal is obvious. It's like having a backing band that fits into your pocket and doesn't mind listening to you solo for hours on end! Despite this, many don't think to use backing tracks as a regular practice tool or don't incorporate them as effectively as they could in their practice.

Sometimes, improving our skill at something isn't necessarily about the amount of time we spend; it's about how we spend our time. Practicing guitar in smaller *bite-sized* chunks can be a very effective way to concentrate on different elements of our playing. As guitarists, we tend to fall into the trap of playing a lot without really *practicing* anything. While mindless meandering around the fretboard isn't always a bad thing, it doesn't train us to be musical in our phrasing, expression, and feel.

Practicing in the context of a song forces us to think more about what we're playing. We have to listen to what we're doing to create something that sounds musically coherent. We don't just want to practice playing isolated licks and scales; we also want to practice *hearing* them in context. As such, jam tracks can help cultivate an awareness of what's happening around us when we play and train us to be sensitive to things like feel and timing. Developing solid rhythm and an ear for dynamics comes from playing with other musicians. Using high-quality backing tracks is a convenient way to simulate this experience.

The audio that accompanies this handbook aims to provide an engaging musical backdrop for practicing. (There's nothing less inspiring than jamming to something that sounds like it came pre-loaded on an old electric piano.) This collection of jam tracks draws on influences from rock, pop, blues, and folk. It was put together to span a number of key signatures, both major and minor. Although the songs aim to have a cohesive sound, they intentionally vary in feel and tempo. Experimenting with different keys and tempos ensures that we're continually widening our comfort zone on the fretboard.

As suggested in the book title, each backing track is approximately 5 minutes long. These short time frames accommodate using various songs within a single practice session. For example, if you have 25 minutes per day to practice, this time could be spent working through a handful of jam tracks. This would provide far more focus than just mindlessly noodling on autopilot for half an hour.

Not only is this a more constructive way to use your practice time, it also offers the added benefit of breaking down this time into smaller sections. These 5-minute chunks can be used much like timed training drills to concentrate on the specific areas of your playing that require attention.

Note: Before getting started, be sure to access your free online bonus material. To grab your jam tracks and bonus downloads, head to: **www.guitariq.com/5mj-bonus**

Structure & Mindset

Before looking at the specific jam tracks accompanying this handbook, let's discuss some general concepts for using backing tracks effectively in our practice time.

Thinking About Focus

When given the opportunity to play over a chord progression, the immediate temptation for many guitarists is to launch into an endless onslaught of scales and familiar licks. Although aimless noodling can be fun, constantly playing the same old things doesn't provide much opportunity to grow or challenge ourselves creatively. Again, while it may be difficult to practice without playing, it's very easy to play without really *practicing* anything.

One of the recurring concepts in this guide is simply that *focused practice is efficient practice*. This means being more intentional with your practice time. For example, when you sit down to play guitar, how often do you define the exact elements of your playing you're choosing to work on? Think about it. When was the last time you asked yourself: What are my exact objectives for the time I've dedicated to improve my playing today?

When we pick up the guitar, it's a fair assumption for most of us the goal is simply to practice. But practice what? What does that actually mean? Does it mean we're intending to work on our technique, our music theory, or our improvisation? Perhaps it means we want to improve our fretboard visualization, ear training, or songwriting skills? Most likely, it's a general combination of a number of these things, with no clear overall agenda.

Suppose we did actually predefine the focus of a practice session: *improvisation,* for example. What exact aspect of improvisation are we referring to? Do we want to work on our choice of melody and phrasing or our use of dynamics and emotion? Do we want to write some new melodic ideas or nail that difficult lick we can't quite play yet? Are we focused on our fretboard navigation skills or mastering a specific technique, and if so, which one?

While we could continue refining our focus even further, please don't confuse the point of this brief exercise. In truth, all these elements are connected. The intention isn't to overwhelm you with the many ways you could spend your practice time but to do precisely the opposite: to get you focused on the specifics of what you want to improve so your practice will be more effective.

Many guitar players experience the feeling of stunted creativity, like they're stuck playing the same old things and are unsure how to move forward. Identifying the particulars of what you want to improve sets a clear agenda for your practice time. A general desire to become a better guitar player is certainly positive, but it isn't overly *informative*. Articulating the specific skills or techniques you're looking to develop provides a clearer road map for achieving your goals.

> **Tip:** *Often, to move forward in your playing, it's helpful to think backward. Picture the overarching goal or skill set you'd like to achieve and then retrace the smaller steps required for getting there. While these steps will undoubtedly evolve as your knowledge increases, reflecting on this process will help provide clarity and direction for how you spend your practice time.*

Thinking About Structure

Having discussed being more intentional with your practice time, let's consider some specific suggestions for working with the jam tracks provided (or any backing tracks for that matter). Before sitting down to play guitar, think about the time you have and the number of songs you'd like to work through. This will be different for everybody. Some might spend 15 minutes warming up with practice tracks before focusing the rest of their time on learning a new song or, better yet, *writing* a new song. Others might prefer spending an hour or more working exclusively with the jam tracks. How you structure your time is up to you. The point here is to have some kind of *structure* in the first place. Below are some examples of how you might use jam tracks to focus on specific elements of your playing.

Scales

Scales are the building blocks for our melodic vocabulary. Backing tracks are a fantastic way to practice using them, because they add a lot more musicality to a task that can otherwise seem somewhat uninspiring. For those just starting out with scales, it may be helpful to spend an entire song simply looping through one scale shape at a time. You could then switch backing tracks and practice using that scale in a different key—or, alternatively, repeat the track and practice a different position of the same scale. Those a little more experienced could use jam tracks to practice navigating through every position of a scale up and down the entire fretboard in various keys. Always remember, scales don't always have to be played the same way. Try alternating the rhythm to complement the feel of each backing track.

Chords

Chords aren't just important for playing rhythm guitar! As a lead guitarist, having a thorough knowledge of the progression you're playing over is extremely valuable. Understanding the chords being used helps shape our melodic decisions. As chord charts are provided for each song, some may find it helpful to practice playing along, focusing on technique and timing. More advanced players could use the progressions provided and practice coming up with alternative chord voicings or inversions. Experiment with playing each progression in multiple ways, using various positions on the fretboard.

Arpeggios

Arpeggios are essentially *chord shapes* found within the different scales we're using. These shapes can be used melodically to accentuate the chord tones within a particular key. Using jam tracks, less experienced players can practice locating the arpeggio patterns found within the scales they're working on. More experienced players can use jam tracks to practice major and minor arpeggios in all positions on the fretboard at various tempos. Try altering these patterns to include a 7th or 9th for added color. As backing tracks often follow a consistent progression, they're also a fantastic way to practice *playing over the changes*. This means emphasizing the arpeggio shape that corresponds to each specific chord change when improvising over a piece of music.

Technique

Playing technique underpins everything we do on guitar. While *good* technique should be a focus regardless of what's being played, backing tracks can be used to work on specific areas of technique needing development. This applies to players of all skill levels. Perhaps your left hand needs to develop more strength in the little finger, or maybe your picking technique lacks accuracy and speed. It could be you just want to experiment with a skill you haven't mastered yet. Whatever the case, we can use jam tracks to create small training drills and then experiment with applying those exercises in different keys at various tempos. Try repeating the same track, each time focusing on a different element of your playing technique. Execution of fundamental skills such as the use of legato, vibrato, bends, and slides are all good examples of this.

Fretboard Navigation

Fretboard navigation is a fairly broad term. In many ways, it incorporates different elements from each of the previous examples. Simply put, backing tracks can help extend our use of fretboard real estate when playing in particular keys. This could involve navigating through scales and arpeggios in every position on the guitar neck, or learning how various scale patterns and chord shapes overlap one another in a single playing position. In either situation, *visualization* is an important concept. Being able to clearly visualize the way things are connected on the fretboard helps us apply this information with more fluency. Experiment with playing similar melodic ideas in different positions on the guitar neck. Focus on how the tone and feel changes even though the notes may stay the same.

Improvisation

Improvisation is more than making something up on the spot; it's about expressing yourself through your instrument. Jam tracks are obviously an essential tool for working on this ability. Use your practice time to break down the specifics of this skill. Repeat the same jam track several times, each time focusing on a different element of your playing. Use of dynamics, phrasing, and melody are all examples of this. Try experimenting with alternate scales or the use of *chromatic notes*. See if you can sing the melody you're playing, while you're playing it. Perhaps challenge yourself to use only two or three notes for an entire song. Maybe even limit yourself to playing on just one string. Often, mixing things up or working within self-imposed limitations helps us see things in a new way. As with all these examples, the secret to being creative is simply learning to *think creatively*!

The 5-Minute Mindset

Now that we've covered a number of suggestions for using jam tracks more productively, the real goal is to get you thinking for yourself. Other ways to structure your practice time might include the use of specific warm-up exercises, drills for developing speed, learning new licks to add to your musical vocabulary, and so on. There are no rules here! It's about experimentation and finding what works for you.

To clarify, please note that the concept here isn't to *only* practice certain skills in isolation. There's little point becoming proficient at playing particular scales or arpeggios if we don't practice using them in our improvisation or songwriting. Integrating different concepts and techniques is therefore extremely important. The end goal is for all elements of our playing to work together seamlessly. Becoming more deliberate with our practice time also doesn't mean there shouldn't be room for spontaneity in our practice structure. Spontaneity is an important part of creativity. The structures we create for ourselves exist to serve our creativity, not hinder it.

To reiterate, the central point is developing the ability to break things down into their smaller components in order to clearly define our focus. While this doesn't necessarily require the use of jam tracks, they not only offer a more musical context for practicing but also provide short, concentrated blocks in which to structure our time. Again, playing in context and thinking intentionally will help ensure we're maximizing our effort.

Ultimately, the idea of this *5-minute* mindset isn't really concerned with the actual number of minutes spent concentrating on any given task. It's about having a clear system for developing and reflecting on the various elements that contribute to our playing ability as a whole. This is the simple, yet powerful, premise behind **5-Minute Guitar Jams**.

Tip: Learning guitar isn't a sprint. Pace yourself. Don't become so overwhelmed with all the ways you could improve your playing that you end up working on none of them! Narrow your focus and concentrate on those things that align with your specific goals.

Tips for Improvisation

As one last stop before picking up the guitar, let's focus on some central insights concerning improvisation. The numerous benefits of incorporating jam tracks into our practice have already been outlined in this chapter. While backing tracks shouldn't be seen exclusively as a tool for improvising, improvisation does warrant special attention. Why? Because it provides a valuable critique on our playing as a whole. Improvisation requires that our playing technique, skills at fretboard navigation, and musical intuition all work together. It's also an immediate and effective way to experiment with new patterns, techniques, and concepts. Beyond this, most importantly, it's fun!

Improvisation, by its very nature, is defined by spontaneity; it's a free-form musical expression. As such, it's difficult to definitively outline a *correct* approach to improvising over a piece of music. Creativity, after all, is completely subjective! Having said that, if we're looking to craft solos that are just as enjoyable to listen to as they are to play, there are some fundamental concepts that recur across many genres and playing styles.

Improvisation, like all aspects of learning guitar, is a skill that needs to be practiced. Finding your own voice on the guitar requires learning how to speak the language of music fluently. As you work through these backing tracks, here are some key points worth considering:

- **Think Melody First:** A keen sense of melody is the difference between sounding like you're playing scales and sounding like you're playing *music*. Concentrating on melody brings focus to your musical ideas and creates a more engaging interaction with the listener.

- **Emotion Is Key:** The feel and emotion of *how* something is played say equally as much as what's played. Sometimes, simpler musical ideas played with feeling communicate significantly more than overly complex phrases, regardless of the technical proficiency they may require.

- **Focus on Dynamics:** Dynamics are a central channel through which feeling is conveyed. They encompass a wide range of sonic variances: loud, soft, simple, complex, tense, resolved, fast, and slow, for example. A dynamic performance will draw on various modes of expression.

- **Concentrate on Phrasing:** Melodic ideas should communicate something. Sensitivity to phrasing is what separates non-musical meanderings from coherent musical statements. Think about improvisation in terms of a *conversation*, where melodic statements are made and then responded to.

- **Make Use of Repetition:** Establishing, revisiting, and embellishing similar melodic themes throughout a song are key tools in songwriting. Not only does this type of repetition provide more mileage from a single melodic idea, but it also introduces structure and familiarity into a performance.

- **Be Sensitive to Space:** We often have a tendency to overplay, to fill up every space between phrases. This can confuse the main melodic ideas we're trying to express and become quite tiresome to listen to. Often, what you *don't* play says just as much as what you do play.

- **Technique Is a Tool:** Ultimately, technique should support musicality, not replace it. It's easy to develop an unbalanced fascination with speed and other technical aspects of guitar playing. While efficient and accurate technique is essential, it should never be the end goal itself.

- **Don't Ignore Theory:** While theory is no substitute for creativity, it provides the foundation for it. Understanding the essentials of how chords and scales are related will shape the essence of your musical vocabulary. Music theory informs and underpins everything we do on guitar.

- **Practice Creativity:** Creativity is a way of thinking. Train yourself to play with your *ears*, not your fingers. Our fingers always gravitate toward the familiar patterns and ideas they're used to playing. Try to practice hearing melodic ideas in your head before you play them on the fretboard.

- **Remember to Listen:** For a musician, *listening* is as important as playing. Music has an innate ability to tell you where it needs to go. Paying careful attention to the movement and instrumentation surrounding what you play will help ensure that a song sounds cohesive as a whole.

2

5-Minute Jams

Now that we've discussed some central concepts for working with backing tracks, let's take an in-depth look at the jam tracks accompanying this guide.

Using This Handbook

In this chapter, we'll now shift focus from the conceptual to the practical. The following sections directly accompany the audio that's provided with this handbook. While much of this content will hopefully be self-explanatory, it may be helpful to briefly summarize the information provided.

This chapter outlines several chord progressions relating to specific key signatures. Basic track information is noted at the beginning of each section. This includes the key, time signature, and tempo of each jam track. In reference to the accompanying audio, the track number of each song is also provided.

The listed scales and arpeggios under *Primary Options* refer to popular patterns often used when playing over progressions in that key. The numbered sequences in the brackets alongside each suggestion (e.g., R - 3 - 5 - 7) refer to how that pattern relates to the structure of its parent major or minor scale. Below are examples of these patterns in the keys of C major and A minor.

Example 2.1

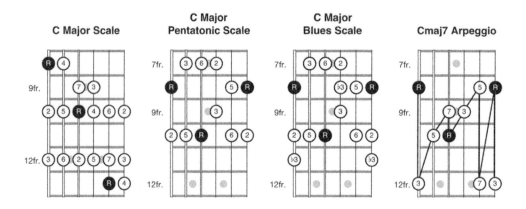

Example 2.2

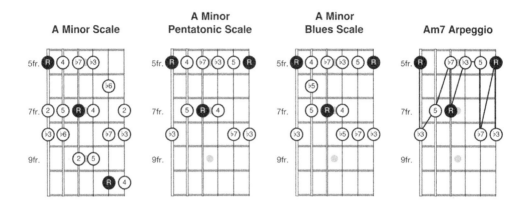

A Minor Scale | A Minor Pentatonic Scale | A Minor Blues Scale | Am7 Arpeggio

> **Tip:** These examples highlight how multiple patterns can be interchangeable within a single position on the fretboard. Although these shapes are a great starting point, it's important to remember that each scale and arpeggio pattern can be played in numerous ways across the guitar neck (please refer to **Chapter 3**).

The options under *Additional Suggestions* highlight a couple of other alternatives you could incorporate into your improvisation. While this isn't meant to be an exhaustive list, these represent some secondary options to experiment with. Typically, these patterns will sound less *resolved* than the primary ones, but they can be easily merged into melodic ideas for added interest and tonal character.

Importantly, the numbered sequences in brackets alongside these secondary suggestions (e.g., 3 - 5 - 7 - 9) refer to how each pattern relates to the specific key we might be playing over. In other words, these numbers highlight the *intervals* each pattern will accent in regards to the parent major or minor scale of the key. They don't refer to the internal structure of the specific pattern itself.

Note: Underlined numbers (e.g., R - 2 - ♭3 - 3 - 5 - 6) show those notes outside the diatonic structure of the key we're playing in. These chromatic notes are considered to be *passing tones* because they aren't found within the key center we're playing in.

Finally, neck diagrams and guitar TAB relating to each progression are also provided. For simplicity, the included TAB is a demonstration of the progression used, not a transcription of the entire jam track. For those working with the suggested audio accompaniment, these charts represent how each progression was recorded. Others preferring to use this handbook by itself can interpret information such as tempo and strumming patterns to taste.

Track List

Below you'll find a track list of each jam track provided:

1. C Major Jam

2. A Minor Jam

3. A Major Jam

4. F# Minor Jam

5. G Major Jam

6. E Minor Jam

7. E Major Jam

8. C# Minor Jam

9. D Major Jam

10. B Minor Jam

C Major Jam

Track Information

- Track Number: 01

- Key Signature: C major

- Time Signature: 4 / 4

- Tempo: 85 BPM

Primary Options

- Cmaj7 arpeggio (R - 3 - 5 - 7)

- C major scale (R - 2 - 3 - 4 - 5 - 6 - 7)

- C major pentatonic scale (R - 2 - 3 - 5 - 6)

- C major blues scale (R - 2 - ♭3 - 3 - 5 - 6)

Additional Suggestions

- Em7 arpeggio (3 - 5 - 7 - 9)

- G major blues scale (5 - 6 - ♭7 - 7 - 2 - 3)

Chord Diagrams

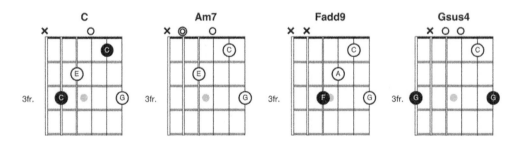

Chord Progression

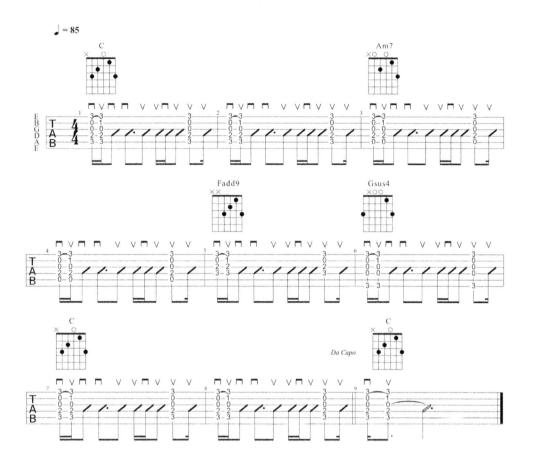

A Minor Jam

Track Information

- Track Number: 02

- Key Signature: A minor

- Time Signature: 4 / 4

- Tempo: 115 BPM

Primary Options

- Am7 arpeggio (R - ♭3 - 5 - ♭7)

- A minor scale (R - 2 - ♭3 - 4 - 5 - ♭6 - ♭7)

- A minor pentatonic scale (R - ♭3 - 4 - 5 - ♭7)

- A minor blues scale (R - ♭3 - 4 - ♭5 - 5 - ♭7)

Additional Suggestions

- Cmaj7 arpeggio (♭3 - 5 - ♭7 - 9)

- E minor blues scale (5 - ♭7 - R - ♭2 - 2 - 4)

Chord Diagrams

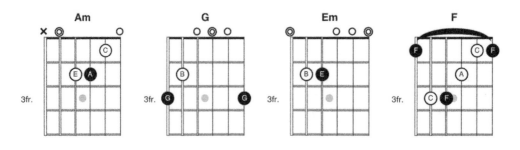

Chord Progression

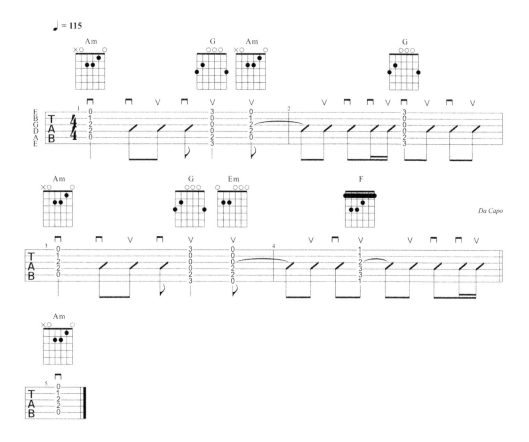

A Major Jam

Track Information

- Track Number: 03

- Key Signature: A major

- Time Signature: 4 / 4

- Tempo: 70 BPM

Primary Scales

- Amaj7 arpeggio (R - 3 - 5 - 7)

- A major scale (R - 2 - 3 - 4 - 5 - 6 - 7)

- A major pentatonic scale (R - 2 - 3 - 5 - 6)

- A major blues scale (R - 2 - ♭3 - 3 - 5 - 6)

Additional Suggestions

- C#m7 arpeggio (3 - 5 - 7 - 9)

- E major blues scale (5 - 6 - ♭7 - 7 - 2 - 3)

Chord Diagrams

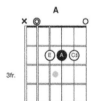
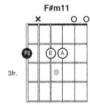
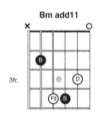
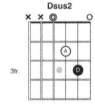
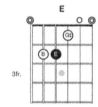

Chord Progression

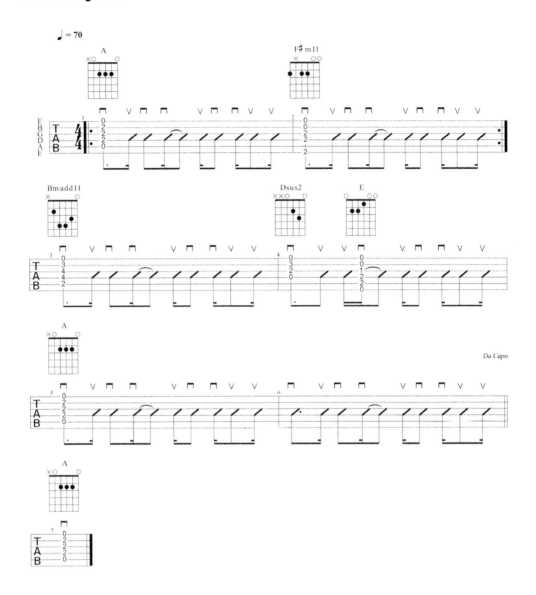

F# Minor Jam

Track Information

- Track Number: 04

- Key Signature: F# minor

- Time Signature: 6 / 8

- Tempo: 100 BPM

Primary Options

- F#m7 arpeggio (R - ♭3 - 5 - ♭7)

- F# minor scale (R - 2 - ♭3 - 4 - 5 - ♭6 - ♭7)

- F# minor pentatonic scale (R - ♭3 - 4 - 5 - ♭7)

- F# minor blues scale (R - ♭3 - 4 - <u>♭5</u> - 5 - ♭7)

Additional Suggestions

- Amaj7 arpeggio (♭3 - 5 - ♭7 - 9)

- C# minor blues scale (5 - ♭7 - R - <u>♭2</u> - 2 - 4)

Chord Diagrams

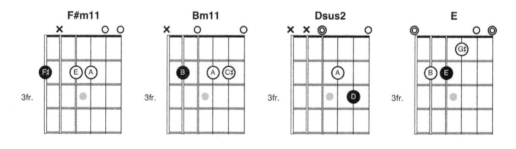

Chord Progression

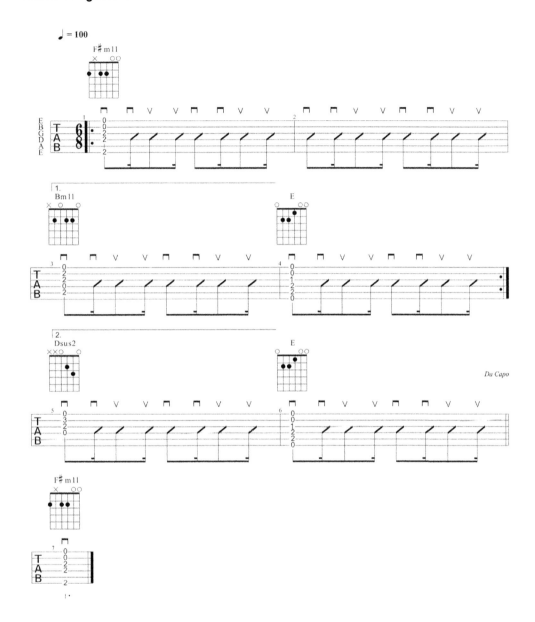

G Major Jam

Track Information

- Track Number: 05

- Key Signature: G major

- Time Signature: 4 / 4

- Tempo: 80 BPM

Primary Options

- Gmaj7 arpeggio (R - 3 - 5 - 7)

- G major scale (R - 2 - 3 - 4 - 5 - 6 - 7)

- G major pentatonic scale (R - 2 - 3 - 5 - 6)

- G major blues scale (R - 2 - ♭3 - 3 - 5 - 6)

Additional Suggestions

- Bm7 arpeggio (3 - 5 - 7 - 9)

- D major blues scale (5 - 6 - ♭7 - 7 - 2 - 3)

Chord Diagrams

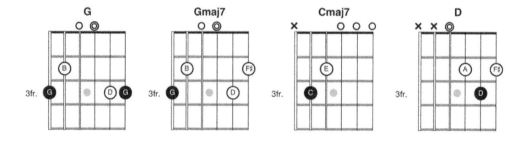

Chord Progression

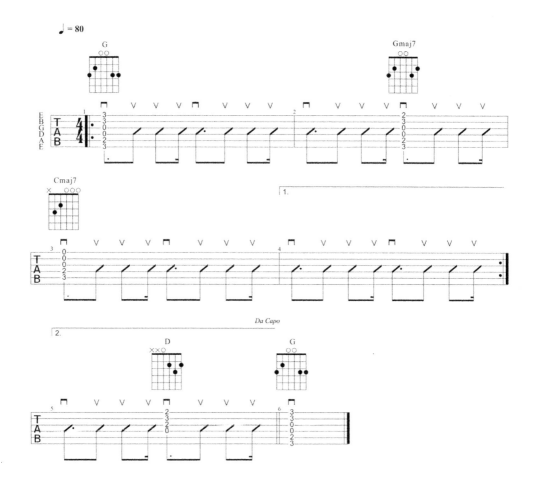

E Minor Jam

Track Information

- Track Number: 06

- Key Signature: E minor

- Time Signature: 4 / 4

- Tempo: 90 BPM

Primary Options

- Em7 arpeggio (R - ♭3 - 5 - ♭7)

- E minor scale (R - 2 - ♭3 - 4 - 5 - ♭6 - ♭7)

- E minor pentatonic scale (R - ♭3 - 4 - 5 - ♭7)

- E minor blues scale (R - ♭3 - 4 - ♭5 - 5 - ♭7)

Additional Suggestions

- Gmaj7 arpeggio (♭3 - 5 - ♭7 - 9)

- B minor blues scale (5 - ♭7 - R - ♭2 - 2 - 4)

Chord Diagrams

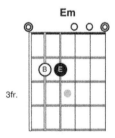
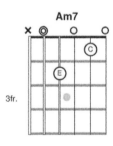
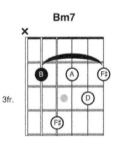

Chord Progression

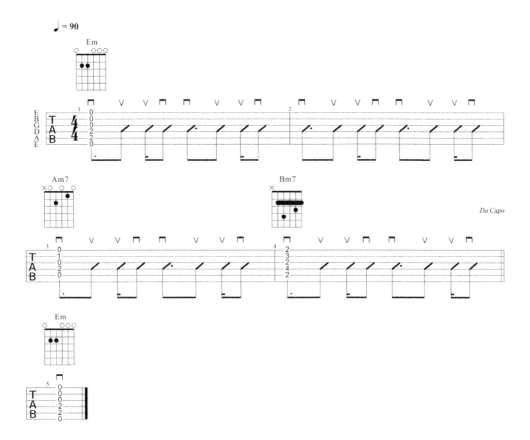

E Major Jam

Track Information

- Track Number: 07

- Key Signature: E major

- Time Signature: 4 / 4

- Tempo: 95 BPM

Primary Options

- Emaj7 arpeggio (R - 3 - 5 - 7)

- E major scale (R - 2 - 3 - 4 - 5 - 6 - 7)

- E major pentatonic scale (R - 2 - 3 - 5 - 6)

- E major blues scale (R - 2 - ♭3 - 3 - 5 - 6)

Additional Suggestions

- G♯m7 arpeggio (3 - 5 - 7 - 9)

- B major blues scale (5 - 6 - ♭7 - 7 - 2 - 3)

Chord Diagrams

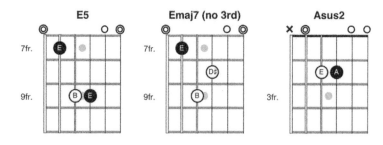

Chord Progression

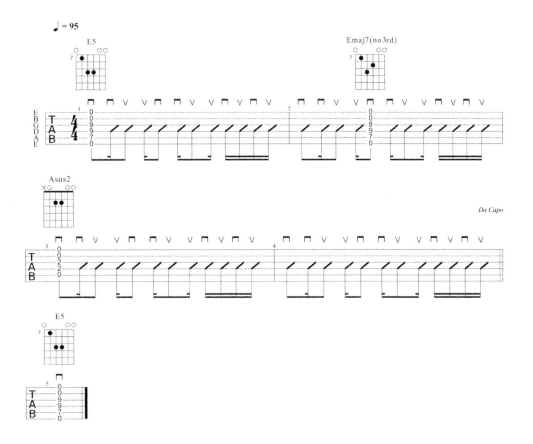

C# Minor Jam

Track Information

- Track Number: 08

- Key Signature: C# minor

- Time Signature: 4 / 4

- Tempo: 105 BPM

Primary Options

- C#m7 arpeggio (R - ♭3 - 5 - ♭7)

- C# minor scale (R - 2 - ♭3 - 4 - 5 - ♭6 - ♭7)

- C# minor pentatonic scale (R - ♭3 - 4 - 5 - ♭7)

- C# minor blues scale (R - ♭3 - 4 - ♭5 - 5 - ♭7)

Additional Suggestions

- Emaj7 arpeggio (♭3 - 5 - ♭7 - 9)

- G# minor blues scale (5 - ♭7 - R - ♭2 - 2 - 4)

Chord Diagrams

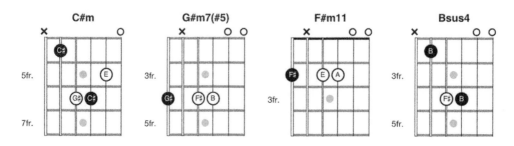

Chord Progression

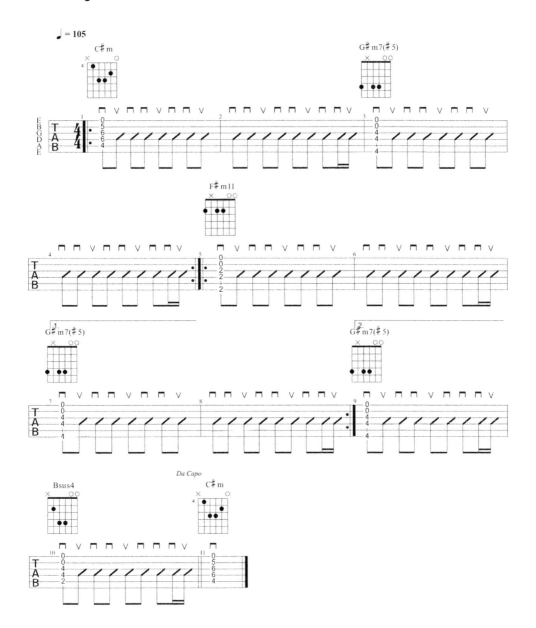

D Major Jam

Track Information

- Track Number: 09

- Key Signature: D major

- Time Signature: 4 / 4

- Tempo: 110 BPM

Primary Options

- Dmaj7 arpeggio (R - 3 - 5 - 7)

- D major scale (R - 2 - 3 - 4 - 5 - 6 - 7)

- D major pentatonic scale (R - 2 - 3 - 5 - 6)

- D major blues scale (R - 2 - ♭3 - 3 - 5 - 6)

Additional Suggestions

- F#m7 arpeggio (3 - 5 - 7 - 9)

- A major blues scale (5 - 6 - ♭7 - 7 - 2 - 3)

Chord Diagrams

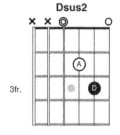
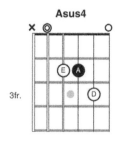
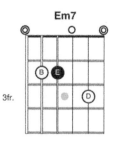
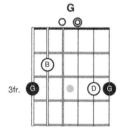

Chord Progression

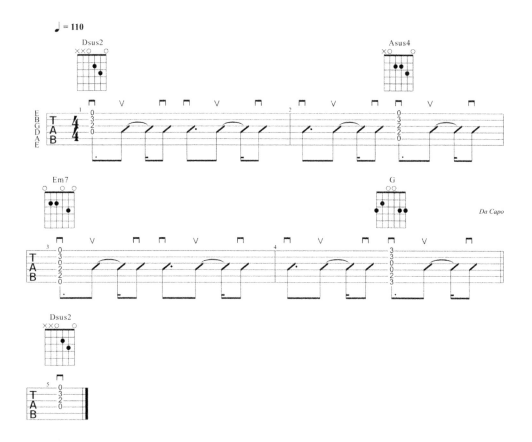

B Minor Jam

Track Information

- Track Number: 10

- Key Signature: B minor

- Time Signature: 4 / 4

- Tempo: 75 BPM

Primary Options

- Bm7 arpeggio (R - ♭3 - 5 - ♭7)

- B minor scale (R - 2 - ♭3 - 4 - 5 - ♭6 - ♭7)

- B minor pentatonic scale (R - ♭3 - 4 - 5 - ♭7)

- B minor blues scale (R - ♭3 - 4 - ♭5 - 5 - ♭7)

Additional Suggestions

- Dmaj7 arpeggio (♭3 - 5 - ♭7 - 9)

- F♯ minor blues scale (5 - ♭7 - R - ♭2 - 2 - 4)

Chord Diagrams

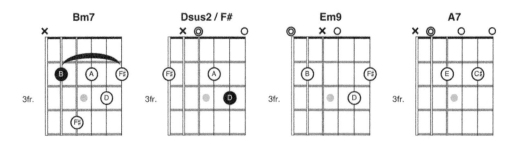

Chord Progression

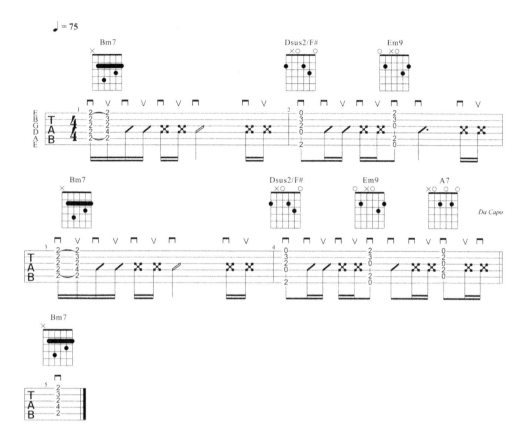

3

Quick Navigation Guide

Having referenced various scale shapes and arpeggio patterns, we'll now briefly explore how these options relate to the fretboard.

Visualizing Scales

The previous chapter took an in-depth look at the jam tracks accompanying this handbook. A lot of information was covered here, including numerous scale and arpeggio suggestions. While this handbook isn't intended to be a comprehensive guide for using scales, it seems fitting to conclude with demonstrating the key shapes and positions that have been discussed.

Throughout this guide, we've referred to four main pattern types for the purpose of improvisation. Again, these suggestions don't include all the options available to us when improvising or songwriting, but they do represent foundational patterns that span numerous genres. To reiterate, these are:

- major/minor scales

- major/minor pentatonic scales

- major/minor blues scales

- major/minor seventh arpeggios

In the following sections, we'll demonstrate what each pattern looks like in their various positions on the fretboard. Rather than outlining each shape in isolation, the intention is to show how they relate to one another. As such, the following diagrams are grouped not by their type but by their relative *position* on the fretboard.

Because pentatonic scales are a familiar starting point for many guitar players, we'll use the five positions of the pentatonic scale to reference our relative position on the fretboard. Notice the unique shapes created by the root notes in each set of patterns. Even though the shape of each pattern changes, the structure of the root notes does not. Practice using these *octave shapes* to reference the scales and arpeggios that are connected to them. (This concept is often referenced as part of the CAGED system.)

Lastly, these patterns are all *movable* shapes. While we'll be using the keys of C major and A minor for the following examples, these patterns can be applied to any key. If we're playing in B minor, for example, each A minor pattern would simply shift up a whole step.

Tip: *Hopefully, many of the following shapes will be familiar to you. When learning new patterns, however, it's important to be conscious of information overload. Work with the backing tracks, and concentrate on each new shape, one at a time, before moving on to the next. Don't rush! It's far better knowing a few positions really well than knowing many of them poorly.*

Note: This chapter is intended to be a quick reference guide for visualizing the various patterns that have been discussed. For more comprehensive lessons on fretboard navigation, theory, and technique please refer to my book **Lead Guitar Breakthrough**.

Major Scales & Arpeggios

Example 3.1

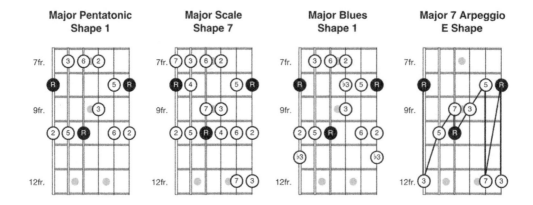

Example 3.2

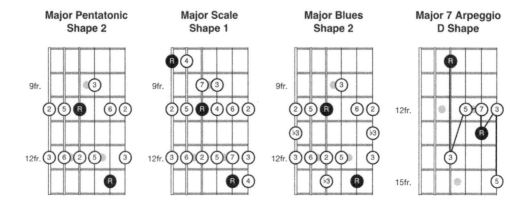

Example 3.3

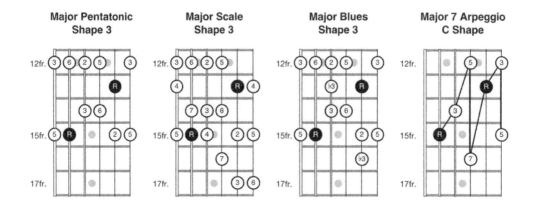

Example 3.4

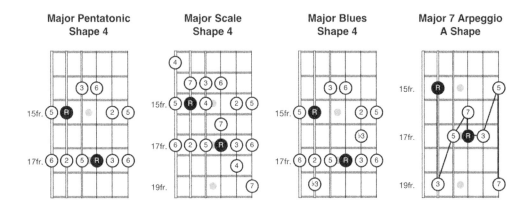

Example 3.5

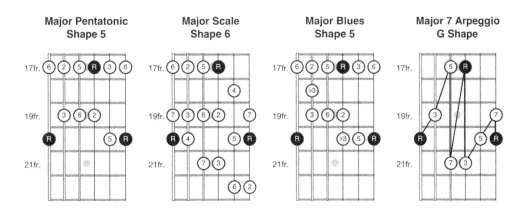

Minor Scales & Arpeggios

Example 3.6

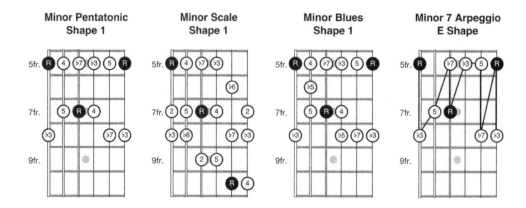

Example 3.7

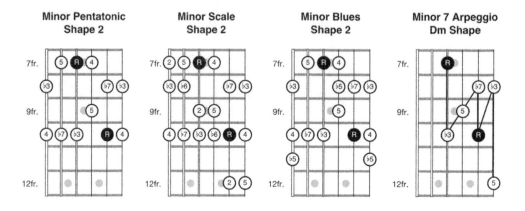

Example 3.8

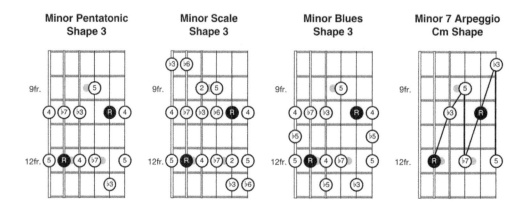

Example 3.9

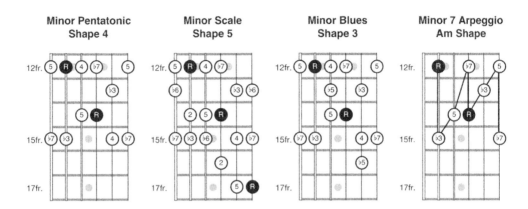

Minor Pentatonic
Shape 4

Minor Scale
Shape 5

Minor Blues
Shape 3

Minor 7 Arpeggio
Am Shape

Example 3.10

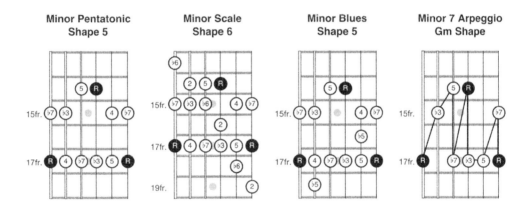

Minor Pentatonic
Shape 5

Minor Scale
Shape 6

Minor Blues
Shape 5

Minor 7 Arpeggio
Gm Shape

Final Thoughts

Congratulations on completing **5-Minute Guitar Jams**!

This handbook was written as a companion to those looking for a greater sense of motivation and direction in their practice time. Throughout this guide, we've focused on two key concepts: playing *in context* and practicing with *intention*. Accordingly, jam tracks have been emphasized repeatedly as an effective method for promoting both ideas.

To summarize, practicing in the context of a song places our playing pursuits, both creative and technical, into a more realistic musical environment. We're forced to experiment with various keys and tempos, listen in greater detail to what we're playing, and be sensitive to the instrumentation around us. Practicing in repetitive bite-sized chunks allows us to narrow down our focus to the particular elements of our playing we're looking to improve. In this way, being intentional with our focus maximizes the effectiveness of our time and effort.

It's been the goal of this handbook not only to provide helpful material to use when practicing but, more importantly, to offer a fresh way of thinking about practicing. Sometimes, even small adjustments can produce big results. I hope this simple guide will be a valuable reference as you continue to work through both the jam tracks provided and the future practice material you'll encounter.

May this book help inspire you toward continued learning and creativity.

Liked This Bundle?

Did you find this bundle useful? You can make a big difference in helping us spread the word!

While it would be nice to have the promotional muscle of a major publishing house, independent authors rely heavily on the loyalty of their audience. Online reviews are one of the most powerful tools we have for getting attention and finding new readers.

If you found this bundle helpful, please consider helping us by leaving a review at your place of purchase. Reviews needn't be long or in-depth; a star rating with a short comment is perfect. If you could take a minute to leave your feedback, it would be sincerely appreciated!

Additional Resources

For more resources, including great free content, be sure to visit us at:

www.guitariq.com

Stay in touch with all the latest news. To connect with us online, head to:

www.guitariq.com/connect

Would you like to read more? For a complete list of Luke's books, check out:

www.guitariq.com/books

Remember to grab your online bonus! Get the bonus content for this bundle at:

www.guitariq.com/lgbb-bonus

Interested in a master class with Luke? To check out his online workshops, go to:

www.guitariq.com/academy

About the Author

Having played for over 25 years, Luke Zecchin is an accomplished guitarist with a wealth of studio and live experience. Outside his work teaching music, Luke has toured extensively alongside renowned national and international acts, performing at everything from clubs, theaters, and festivals to various appearances on commercial radio and national television.

Playing lead guitar, Luke has worked on projects with established international producers and engineers. He has been fortunate to see these collaborations break into both the Top 50 ARIA Album and Singles charts, having also received nationwide airplay and notable debuts on the Australian iTunes Rock charts.

As the founder of **GuitarIQ.com**, Luke is dedicated to the education and coaching of guitar players all over the globe. With books available in over 100 countries worldwide, he has emerged as an international chart-topping author in his field.

Luke continues to work as an author and musician from his project studio based in the Adelaide Hills, South Australia.

Find him online at **LukeZecchin.com**.